The Game We Knew

Also by Mike Leonetti and Harold Barkley:
The Game We Knew: Hockey in the Fifties

The Game We Knew

HOCKEY IN THE SIXTIES

MIKE LEONETTI

PHOTOGRAPHY BY HAROLD BARKLEY

RAINCOAST BOOKS

Vancouver

To all the loyal fans of hockey in the sixties
who helped nurture this great game.

First published in 1998 by

Raincoast Books
8680 Cambie Street
Vancouver, B.C.
V6P 6M9
(604) 323-7100

Visit our web site at: www.raincoast.com

1 2 3 4 5 6 7 8 9 10

CANADIAN CATALOGUING IN PUBLICATION DATA
Leonetti, Mike, 1958-
The game we knew: hockey in the sixties

ISBN 1-55192-198-7

1. National Hockey League – History. 2. National Hockey League – History – Pictorial works. I. Barkley, Harold. II. Title.

GV847.8.N3L462 1998   796.962'64   C98-910409-5

Printed in Hong Kong

THE CANADA COUNCIL | LE CONSEIL DES ARTS
FOR THE ARTS | DU CANADA
SINCE 1957 | DEPUIS 1957

Raincoast Books gratefully acknowledges the support of the
Government of Canada, through the Book Publishing Industry
Development Program, the Canada Council for the Arts and the Department of
Canadian Heritage. We also acknowledge the assistance of the Province of
British Columbia through the British Columbia Arts Council.

CONTENTS

FOREWORD

Like many Canadians who grew up in the forties and fifties, I was a big fan of the Toronto Maple Leafs because of Foster Hewitt. Every Saturday night I would listen to his broadcast of Leafs games, and players such as Syl Apps, Ted Kennedy and Turk Broda became my heroes. I remained a Toronto fan until my family moved from my hometown of Timmins, Ontario, to nearby Schumacher. It was while we lived there that I got a Detroit Red Wings uniform for Christmas one year. I quickly became a follower of the Motor City team, which was developing into a dynasty with players such as Gordie Howe and Ted Lindsay. But when my father decided that education was going to be part of my hockey-playing future, I was off to St. Michael's College in Toronto and into the Maple Leafs development chain.

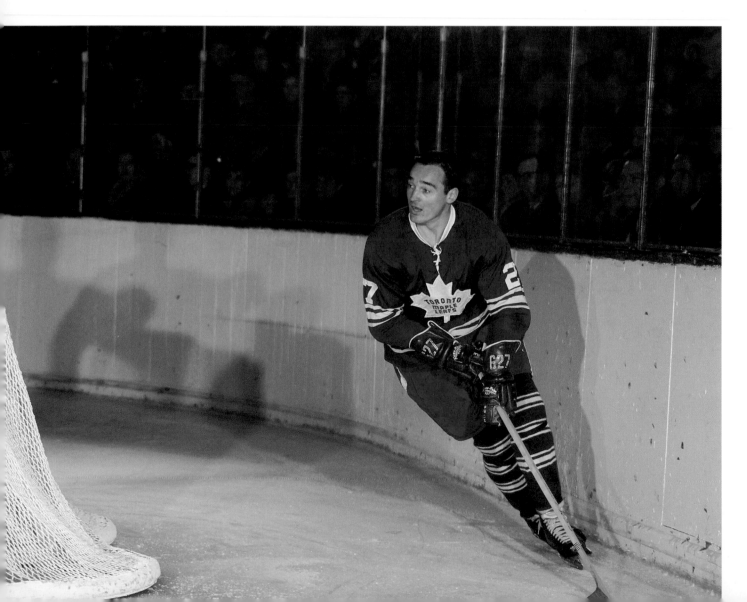

The Leafs of the mid-fifties were not exactly a powerhouse. They could play great defence but had a terrible time scoring goals. Toronto was rebuilding when I came on board, part of a young nucleus of talent, which included Dick Duff, Bob Baun, Bob Pulford and Carl Brewer, to go along with seasoned hands such as George Armstrong, Ron Stewart, Billy Harris and Tim Horton. My rookie season was 1957-58, and I was thrilled to win the Calder Trophy, edging out Bobby Hull, a player I was often compared to in my career. I clearly recall two games from that year. In one I scored my first hat trick, on December 1, 1957, against Chicago's Glenn Hall in a 7-2 win at the Stadium. The other was a three-goal game against the champion Canadiens with Jacques Plante in net at Maple Leaf Gardens on December 25, 1957, in a 5-4 victory.

The first full season of the sixties was also my first big season in the NHL. In 1960-61, when I scored 48 goals, I had a good year in part because of a meeting I had early in the season with coach Punch Imlach. For once he listened to me, and I started to get plenty of ice time. We developed a power play that started to look as good as the one the Canadiens had. I was put at centre (a position I had played in junior) between Bob Nevin and Bert Olmstead, with Red Kelly and Tim Horton on the point, and we really started to click. I had two four-goal games (one against U.S. Olympic hero and Rangers goalie Jack McCartan), and we battled Montreal for first place all season long. But we ran into a number of injuries, and by the end of the year our tank was empty. The Canadiens finished first (92 points to our 90), and the Red Wings knocked us off in just five games during the semifinals.

By this time the Leafs were ready to challenge seriously for the Stanley Cup. We had a good blend of young legs (adding the likes of Dave Keon and Eddie Shack) and veteran savvy from players discarded by other teams (such as Allan Stanley, Johnny Bower, Al Arbour, Ed Litzenberger and Don Simmons). I would have loved to play in a free-wheeling system like the Canadiens had. It would have allowed me to take full advantage of my skating abilities, but there was no changing Imlach's mind. He never knew how to use me properly. Although the coach took the credit for our success, it was really the result of the players deciding as a group that this was our chance to become champions. Imlach wore us down at practice and at the negotiating table, but it was our own determination that carried us to four Stanley Cups in the sixties.

The latter years of the decade of the sixties brought another transition for me. When I got traded by Toronto in March 1968, I was actually relieved. I had stayed in Toronto for too long (I often wonder if I would have been better off going to Chicago in 1962 when that club tried to buy my contract from the Leafs), and I needed a change. I scored 49 goals for Detroit in 1968-69, and I enjoyed my most productive years when I was dealt to Montreal, the classiest organization in hockey. New standards for scoring and offence were established after the expansion in 1967. The Canadiens were ready for the new era of play, whereas teams such as Toronto and Detroit lagged behind, using older players and old methods. It was a pleasure to play for a team that treated me with respect.

New standards for excellence were also being set by photographer Harold Barkley. I can still remember posing for Barkley, and I looked forward to seeing his action shots in the *Star Weekly* magazine. I had one of his photos -- of me fending off Ted Green -- hanging in my office. I am certain, as you look at these classic photos, that they will bring back warm memories of a great time in hockey history.

Frank Mahovlich
Unionville, Ontario
March 1998

INTRODUCTION

Winning the Stanley Cup wasn't supposed to be this easy. But the 1959-60 Montreal Canadiens were hardly an average team. On April 14, 1960, at Maple Leaf Gardens in Toronto, the Canadiens set out to complete their eight-game sweep to the Cup (the Cup had been won in eight straight only once before, by the Detroit Red Wings, and such a sweep would never happen again). Even though the Maple Leafs were down three games to none and clearly overmatched, they fought valiantly to avenge their loss to the Canadiens in the finals the year before. But the Canadiens opened the scoring. Jean Béliveau and Doug Harvey scored goals 28 seconds apart in the first period. Tempers ran high when Bob Pulford ran over Canadiens goalie Jacques Plante and later when Harvey flattened Leafs captain George Armstrong with a crunching bodycheck. Referee Eddie Powers had a difficult time controlling the feisty players.

In the second period, the Maple Leafs went on the attack but could not get the puck past Plante, who foiled Frank Mahovlich on a breakaway from the blueline for his best save of the period. Toronto continued to press, but, with just under four minutes to play in the middle frame, Henri Richard took a pass from Dickie Moore and broke over centre ice with his brother Maurice, the Rocket, on his wing. The younger Richard passed the puck to the Rocket at the Leafs blueline. The Rocket cut into the middle of the ice while keeping the puck away from Leafs defenceman Carl Brewer. Henri broke for the Leafs net, with Toronto's other defenceman, Bobby Baun, in close pursuit. The Rocket slid a crisp pass to Henri, who put the puck past a startled Johnny Bower. The goal made the score 3-0 and put an end to Toronto's comeback hopes. "The Richards combined there for a perfect goal," said broadcaster Foster Hewitt (who was doing the television colour commentary while son Bill did the play-by-play account).

A goal by Béliveau early in the third period made the score 4-0, and Plante kept all shots out of the Canadiens net, clinching Montreal's record fifth straight Stanley Cup. Between 1956 and 1960, the Habs won an amazing 20 of 25 games played in the Stanley Cup finals.

Maurice Richard's assist on his brother's goal proved to be his last playoff point in an illustrious career. Maurice never played another NHL game, retiring with the most ever playoff goals (82;

his last came on a backhand shot past Bower in the third game of the 1960 series) and the most-ever playoff points (a remarkable 126 in 133 games). At the game's end, he accepted the Stanley Cup as Canadiens captain from league president Clarence Campbell. The Rocket spoke briefly in English and then in French, and he posed only with Plante for photos (the rest of his team-mates had left the ice) as they put their arms around each other and the Cup. A Gardens attendant took the Cup away on a table (presumably to be delivered to the Canadiens dressing room), and the Rocket skated off the ice and into the history books.

Here ended the Canadiens dynasty. For the next five years, the team endured a Stanley Cup "drought" as the Maple Leafs assumed the role of NHL champion. But the 1960 finals began a decade-long dominance of the league by the two Canadian teams. Between them, they captured the Stanley Cup in 1960, 1962, 1963, 1964, 1965, 1966, 1967, 1968 and 1969. Professional hockey's greatest rivalry reached its zenith in the sixties, and it would never reach such heights again.

Toronto rebuilt its team in the late fifties under taskmaster coach and general manager Punch Imlach and began to challenge the Montreal powerhouse as early as 1959, when the Maple Leafs lost the finals in a five-game series to the Canadiens. The Habs

The Maple Leafs celebrate Jim Pappin's game-winning goal against Canadiens netminder Gump Worsley in game six of the 1967 finals.

"The only way to beat the Canadiens is to ram it down their throats."

– Toronto coach Punch Imlach
(Hockey News, *April 29, 1967*)

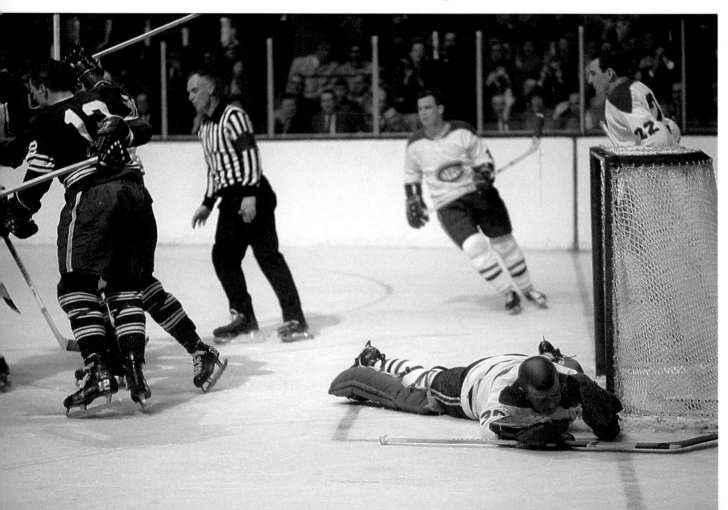

wiped the Leafs out in four straight in 1960, but only a 1961 Chicago title was in the way before Toronto won three in a row. Led by Frank Mahovlich, Dave Keon, Allan Stanley, Tim Horton, Red Kelly and Johnny Bower, the defensively tight Leafs shut down the firepower of the Canadiens for a number of years as the Montreal team added new talent. Holdovers Jean Béliveau, Claude Provost and Henri Richard were joined by rising stars such as Yvan Cournoyer, Jacques Laperriere, Bobby Rousseau, J. C. Tremblay, Gump Worsley, Jacques Lemaire and Serge Savard to win four Cups in five years. The Montreal teams of the late sixties helped to set up another Habs dynasty in the seventies, whereas the Leafs never rejoined the elite of the NHL.

Perhaps that's why the epic battles of the sixties between the two clubs are so fondly remembered by hockey fans. Seeds of rivalry planted in the forties and fifties reached full bloom in the sixties, especially with the games now on television (often on Wednesday nights). These games were exciting to watch, and the players on both sides knew better than anyone else that these contests were something special. French versus English, Quebec versus Ontario, these themes only served to heighten the battles between the two clubs. The close statistics indicate how well the two teams were matched and how important the games were to both cities. From 1960-61 to the end of the 1966-67 season, the Canadiens and Leafs met in 98 regular season games, with Montreal holding a slight edge of 42 wins to Toronto's 39, and another 17 games ended in ties. The playoff confrontations were even more ferocious.

Toronto lost the finals in 1960 to Montreal but resoundingly beat the Canadiens in the 1963 semifinal by four games to one. In 1964 the two teams met once again in the first round, and Toronto won a close series by four games to three, the last win coming in the Forum. However, the 1965 playoffs saw the Canadiens return to glory by knocking off the defending-champion Leafs in the semifinals four games to two and again in 1966, shellacking Toronto four games to none in the first round. The final battle of the sixties saw the teams meet once again for the Stanley Cup during Canada's centennial year of 1967, and Toronto took the Cup in six games to win its fourth title of the decade. It brought the playoff-games win-loss record for the sixties to 18-14 in favour of the Canadiens. It also gave Toronto its 13th Stanley Cup (including championships won by the St. Patrick's and the Arenas, franchise nicknames prior to Maple Leafs) to Montreal's 14 titles (including its Cup win in 1915-16, prior to the formation of the NHL in 1917). The rivalry couldn't have been much closer.

Long-time fans of the Toronto club remember most the 1967 finals, when the Maple Leafs finally got revenge for their loss seven years earlier. Sure, the semifinal wins were satisfying (any win over Montreal was sweet), but nothing could capture the imagination like knowing that an epic battle between the rivals would settle possession of the coveted Stanley Cup. As in 1960, the Leafs were once again the underdog, this time because they were too old!

After a 6-2 loss in the first game at the Forum, it looked like history might repeat itself for the Leafs. They looked weary after taking six games to beat first-place Chicago (a major upset), whereas the Canadiens were fresh from their four-game sweep of the New York Rangers. However, the resilient Leafs won the second game 3-0 and then took the series lead with a classic 3-2 overtime win in Maple Leaf Gardens on the strength of some outstanding goaltending by Johnny Bower. With Bower hurt just before the start of the fourth game, the Canadiens romped 6-2 to square the series. Back in Montreal, the greatest goalie of the six-team era, Terry Sawchuk, locked the door after giving up the opening goal, and Toronto rallied to win 4-1. The series moved back to Maple Leaf Gardens on May 2, 1967, where the Leafs could have wrapped it up in six games. Toronto carried a 2-0 lead into the third period, but a Canadiens goal made Toronto fans nervous. A relentless Montreal attack was turned back by a stellar Sawchuk and a team commitment to stout defensive play. The Leafs faced one last challenge, in the final minute of the game, before it was all over.

Some accounts of that last minute of play have suggested that Leafs coach Punch Imlach was "sentimental" in sending out his old guard of Red Kelly, Bob Pulford, George Armstrong, Tim Horton and Allan Stanley to protect Sawchuk and a 2-1 lead. Imlach was called many things in his day, but he was a calculating man who knew what he wanted. It was not the time to be sentimental with 55 seconds to go and the face-off in the Leafs end. The Leafs mentor knew that the hardened pros could give him one last Cup. To counter the Leafs lineup, Canadiens coach Toe Blake pulled goaltender Gump Worsley and sent out Jean Béliveau, Yvan Cournoyer, Jim Roberts, John Ferguson, Ralph Backstrom and Jacques Laperriere. As Stanley and Béliveau moved into the face-off circle to take the draw, the tension in Maple Leaf Gardens was excruciating.

In textbook fashion, the grizzled Leafs got the job done. Stanley tied up Béliveau as soon as the puck was dropped. Kelly beat

Cournoyer to the loose puck and passed it up the wing to Pulford, who skated the puck over the Leafs blueline. He then passed the puck to Armstrong, who took it just before the redline. The Leafs captain calmly crossed centre (to avoid icing the puck) and took aim at the empty Canadiens cage. Backstrom dove at Armstrong, and the backpedalling Laperriere tried to block the shot at the Montreal blueline, but their efforts were to no avail. Armstrong's wrist shot hit the back of the abandoned net, and the Leafs had a 3-1 victory clinched with only 47 seconds left to play. At long last, Toronto gained revenge for its losses to Montreal in the finals of 1959 and 1960 (the victory also marked the first time the Leafs had beaten the Canadiens for the Stanley Cup since Bill Barilko's overtime goal in 1951). The captain's marker was the final goal of the Leafs dynasty and the last shining moment for Toronto players such as Armstrong, Pulford, Bower, Horton, Kelly and Stanley. And it was the last great moment for the Toronto franchise, to date.

While Toronto and Montreal had the best teams of the decade, Chicago had the most disappointing team. Led by Bobby Hull, the most dominating player of the early and mid-sixties, the Blackhawks did manage a Stanley Cup win in 1961. It looked like they could dominate for a while with the likes of Stan Mikita, Pierre Pilote and Glenn Hall in addition to Hull, but one playoff upset followed another (though they did make it to the finals in 1962 and 1965). The next closest challenge came from the Detroit Red Wings, with a lineup that featured future Hall of Famers Gordie Howe, Alex Delvecchio, Bill Gadsby and Terry Sawchuk. The Red Wings made four trips to the finals (1961, 1963, 1964, 1966), but the Cup eluded them.

The New York Rangers and the Boston Bruins had an unbreakable lease on the basement of the NHL between 1960 and 1966. But things started to change when the Rangers hired Emile Francis as general manager, and he began to build a contender. He brought in players such as Bob Nevin, Ed Giacomin, Jean Ratelle, Vic Hadfield and Rod Seiling to play alongside Don Marshall, Rod Gilbert, Jim Neilson and Harry Howell. By 1967 the Rangers made the playoffs, and although the Canadiens wiped them out they were now a playoff force. Boston's future improved when, in just one trade with Chicago, the Bruins acquired three quality forwards in Phil Esposito, Ken Hodge and Fred Stanfield. But even more important was the prior acquisition of a prized junior prospect who became the catalyst to building a powerhouse in Boston.

Boston acquired Bobby Orr not only to save the franchise but also to lead the Bruins to their first Stanley Cup in 29 years. Since entering the league in 1966-67 as an 18-year-old rookie, Orr had done everything expected of him and more. Named as the league's best rookie, he continued to marvel by winning the Norris Trophy in 1967-68 while playing in only 46 games (recording 31 points), scoring 21 goals in 1968-69 and then doing the unthinkable by leading the NHL in points in 1969-70, with 120 (33 goals, 87 assists), while still playing defence. His record-breaking performance allowed him to become just the second defenceman in league history to win the Hart Trophy (former Bruin Eddie Shore was the first).

On May 10, 1970, Orr and his teammates had the opportunity to cap a tremendous season with a Stanley Cup title. The Bruins had a lead of three games to none over the St. Louis Blues (in their third year of existence), and the fourth game was being played at the Boston Garden. But the stubborn Blues refused to fold, and the game was deadlocked 3-3 late in the third period when Orr picked up the puck near his own blueline. He proceeded on a solo mission to break the tie before overtime. Only the great Glenn Hall, guarding the Blues net, stopped Orr and sent the game into an extra session.

In overtime, Boston coach Harry Sinden started the forward line of Derek Sanderson, Ed Westfall and Wayne Carleton and the defensive pairing of Don Awrey and Bobby Orr. The Bruins quickly got the puck into the Blues end, where Awrey and Westfall combined to keep the puck along the boards and then managed to get it out to Sanderson, who took a shot that went wide. The puck came to St. Louis forward Larry Keenan on the opposite side, and he had a chance to get the puck out, with Tim Ecclestone and Red Berenson ready to join him in an attack on the Boston net. But Orr gambled and neatly blocked Keenan's clearing attempt, getting the puck to Sanderson, who was now along the boards behind the Blues net.

As soon as Orr made the pass, his superb instincts took him to the front of the net. Sanderson put a perfect pass on Orr's stick, and the Bruins superstar rifled a shot past Hall while being tripped by Blues defenceman Noel Picard. Orr flew through the air like Superman on a mission, and when he landed the Bruins had won the Stanley Cup after just 40 seconds of overtime. Orr was mobbed by his teammates while still lying on the ice, and the Boston Garden rocked like it never had before (or has since). Fittingly, Orr was named as winner of the Conn Smythe Trophy (14 points in 14 playoff games), and he had led the Bruins from worst to first in just four seasons. The Boston victory signalled a new hockey power on the rise, and Orr's dominance heralded a new style of play that would change the nature of the game.

The new era actually had begun in 1967-68, when the league doubled in size by adding the St. Louis Blues, Pittsburgh Penguins, Los Angeles Kings, Minnesota North Stars, Philadelphia Flyers and Oakland Seals. The great expansion gave new opportunities to players buried in the minors and to those who were fringe members of the original six teams. Soon players such as Red Berenson, Les Binkley, Gerry Desjardins, Bernie Parent, Ed Van Impe, Bill White and Gary Smith became synonymous with the Western Division, where all the new teams were housed. All the expansion teams were based in the United States, the beginning of a noticeable trend.

Expansion was not the only major change in hockey during the sixties, as can be seen in the following photographs. Helmets began to appear regularly, especially after the tragic death of Bill Masterton in 1968 from on-ice injuries; curved sticks were fully developed; the face mask was here to stay; defencemen began to join the rush; new uniforms were designed, not only for the expan-

Bobby Orr was at the centre of the Boston Bruins hopes for the future when he joined the team right out of junior hockey in 1966-67.

"Orr is worth $2 million to us because we can build around him for 15 to 20 years and don't think we don't intend to."

– Milt Schmidt, Boston general manager (Hockey Illustrated, *May 6, 1967*)

sion teams but also for the Toronto and Boston clubs; and player power increased with the birth of the Players Association in 1967.

Capturing all the changes was Harold Barkley, who pioneered and refined the art of taking colour action hockey photos. Using a specially designed set of strobe lighting systems that he had developed with a Swedish engineer (and that weighed over 300 pounds), Barkley travelled to the six original NHL cities through most of the sixties. The results were spectacular. His photos have become collector's items, as they were when Barkley first had his work published in the *Star Weekly* magazine, a supplement to the Toronto *Star* newspaper every Saturday. Photos were vital to magazines in the fifties and sixties, and his work certainly helped raise its circulation from 700,000 to over 1 million.

As in *Hockey in the Fifties*, the first volume of *The Game We Knew*, Barkley's photos from the sixties are accompanied by captions, trivia, statistics, marketing and financial data and unusual notes. In addition, this volume has memorable quotations and milestone achievements in the careers of the players and coaches Barkley captured with his bright lights and colour film.

It is appropriate that Barkley is associated with some of the greatest names in hockey—such as Bobby Hull, Gordie Howe, Terry Sawchuk, Glenn Hall, Pierre Pilote, Stan Mikita, Frank Mahovlich, Dave Keon, Norm Ullman, Ed Giacomin, Rod Gilbert, Phil Esposito, Jean Béliveau, Henri Richard and Bobby Orr—because they all helped to make the sixties the most memorable decade in hockey history.

THE PHOTOGRAPHS

JACQUES PLANTE

Montreal goaltender Jacques Plante (#1) was at his best in the 1960 playoffs. In the Canadiens eight-game sweep to the Stanley Cup, he recorded three shutouts, including a 4-0 victory to clinch the finals series against Toronto. A six-time Stanley Cup winner with the Habs, Plante recorded 10 playoff or post-season shutouts with Montreal between 1952 and 1960.

Plante won the Hart Trophy in 1961-62, when he played in 70 games, recording four shutouts and a 2.37 goals-against average. He was the last goalie to win the coveted award until Dominik Hasek of Buffalo won it in 1996-97 with 37 wins and a 2.27 goals-against average in 67 games.

"I thought I proved the mask in the 1960 playoffs when we won eight straight and I scored three shutouts. But every time I'm beaten by what looks like an easy shot to the fans, they say I couldn't see the puck because of the mask."

– Jacques Plante
(Hockey News, *March 10, 1962*)

MARCEL PRONOVOST

Detroit's Marcel Pronovost (#3) tries to put the puck past Toronto goalie Johnny Bower. Pronovost turned professional in 1949-50 with Omaha (in the USHL) and was named the league's best rookie with 13 goals and 52 points while playing defence. He then joined Detroit for the 1950 playoffs, playing in nine postseason games for the Red Wings, who won the Stanley Cup. He was a Red Wing until the end of the 1964-65 season, scoring 80 goals and 297 points in 983 games. Pronovost suffered many injuries in his career, and in the 1961 playoffs he played with a cracked ankle, which he would take out of a cast to play the games. A major off-season trade in May 1965 saw Pronovost go to Toronto, where he captured another Stanley Cup (his fifth) in 1967. He scored his only goal of those playoffs in the fifth game of the finals against Rogie Vachon. His final year was 1968-69, and the two-time first-team all-star (1960, 1961) was elected to the Hall of Fame in 1978.

The Money Game

Marcel Pronovost once earned $5 from Detroit coach and general manager Jack Adams for being the first player on the ice to start the Red Wings training camp of 1957-58 (an annual "bonus" given out by the miserly manager). Prior to the successful lawsuit against the NHL, Pronovost's annual pension income after 21 seasons of play was $9,000. His share of the lawsuit settlement was $102,422.04.

UNUSUAL NOTE

When Detroit manager Jack Adams saw that his club had five days off, he arranged for his Red Wings to play two exhibition games against the Omaha Knights (then in the IHL) for February 13 and 14, 1961.

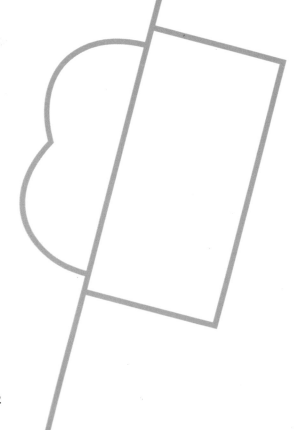

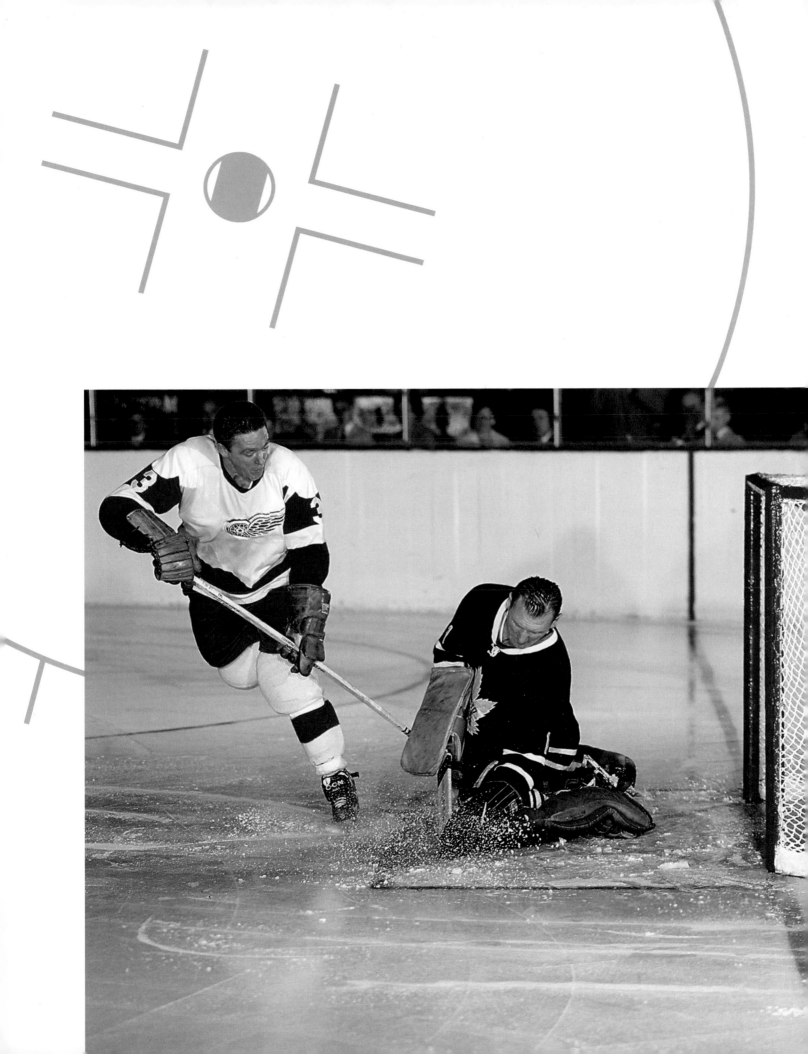

ALLAN STANLEY

Toronto defenceman Allan Stanley (#26) battles for the puck with Boston's Jean-Guy Gendron. The Maple Leafs made a great trade when they acquired Stanley from the Bruins in October 1958. The Leafs sent Jim Morrison to Boston to complete the deal for the longtime NHL veteran, who had also played with New York and Chicago. In Toronto he was paired with Tim Horton and became a three-time all-star (second team in 1960, 1961 and 1966, when he was 40 years old). Stanley tied his career high in goals with 10 in 1959-60 and had a best mark of 35 points in 1961-62, but he was best known as a defensive stalwart during the four Stanley Cup wins for the Leafs in the sixties. His NHL career began in 1948-49 and ended in 1968-69 after one season with the Philadelphia Flyers at the age of 43. Stanley played in 1,244 career games, scoring 100 goals and 433 points. He was elected to the Hall of Fame in 1981.

TRIVIA

Toronto coach and general manager George "Punch" Imlach left both Allan Stanley (33 at the time) and goaltender Johnny Bower (34 at the time) unprotected in the June 1959 intraleague draft, mostly because of age, but luckily for the Maple Leafs neither player was selected. It's a good thing, too, because the replacements Imlach had in mind were Marc Reaume, Al MacNeil (for Stanley), Ed Chadwick and Gerry McNamara (for Bower), none of whom ever made an impact in the NHL as players. It's also highly unlikely that the Leafs would have won four Cups without Stanley and Bower.

UNUSUAL NOTE

Punch Imlach had defencemen take all the face-offs in the Leafs end of the ice during his coaching stint in Toronto. Allan Stanley's most famous face-off victory came against the Canadiens Jean Béliveau in the last game of the 1967 finals with 55 seconds to play and the Leafs clinging to a 2-1 lead. Stanley tied up Béliveau, and the Leafs got the puck out to George Armstrong, who calmly put a shot into the empty Montreal net. It is interesting to note that, with 2:23 to play, Stanley got ready for his confrontation with Béliveau by beating Ralph Backstrom on another key face-off in the Toronto end. The big Leafs defenceman controlled Backstrom while his teammates cleared the zone, setting the stage for Toronto's last stand.

KEN WHARRAM

Chicago's Ken Wharram (#17) has a number of Montreal Canadiens to contend with, including Lou Fontinato (#19), Dickie Moore (#12) and Jacques Plante (#1). Wharram had the best year of his career in 1963-64, when he scored 39 goals and recorded 71 points, both career highs. It earned him the Lady Byng Trophy (only 18 penalty minutes) and a place on the first all-star team. He made another appearance on the first all-star squad in 1966-67, when he finished fourth in league scoring with 65 points (31 goals, 34 assists) and the Blackhawks finished on top of the league for the first time in team history. He was with the Blackhawks in 1961 when they won the Stanley Cup, contributing three goals and five assists in 12 games. Wharram played his entire career in the Chicago organization, retiring after the 1968-69 season with 252 goals and 281 assists.

"From the time I began skating, my goal was to make it to the NHL. I am where I dreamed of being. Sure, there are regrets such as missing Christmas at home with my family now and then, and hockey has taken the best years of my life. However, all I have I owe to this game."

– *Ken Wharram* (Hockey Pictorial, *April/May 1968*)

FIRST GOAL

Ken Wharram scored the first goal of his career on March 19, 1954, in Chicago in a game against the Boston Bruins. In the 7-0 Chicago victory, Wharram scored the final goal of the game and his only tally of the 1953-54 season, when he played in 29 games. He scored his 200th goal on November 12, 1967, when he beat St. Louis Blues goaltender (and former teammate) Glenn Hall in a 5-2 Blackhawks win.

BERNIE GEOFFRION

Montreal's Bernie Geoffrion is knocked into the boards by Detroit's Floyd Smith (#17). Geoffrion scored the biggest goal of his career on March 16, 1961, when he became the second player in NHL history to score 50 goals in one season. He beat Toronto goalie Cesare Maniago in a 5-2 Canadiens victory. "Boom Boom" also led the league in points during 1960-61 with 95, earning him his second Art Ross Trophy. The right winger left hockey after the 1963-64 season but returned to the NHL in 1966-67 with the New York Rangers, scoring 17 goals. In all, Geoffrion scored 393 goals and 429 assists in 883 games.

Floyd Smith played for five NHL teams in his career and scored over 20 goals twice (21 in 1965-66 with Detroit and 24 in 1967-68 with the Red Wings and the Maple Leafs). He was part of one of the biggest deals in NHL history when he was dealt to Toronto with Norm Ullman and Paul Henderson for Frank Mahovlich, Peter Stemkowski, Garry Unger and the rights to Carl Brewer on March 3, 1968.

Marketing the Game

A March 1962 survey showed that 18 companies undertook promotions in Canada with hockey as the theme, often using NHL players in the advertisements. For example, Bob Nevin and Rod Gilbert modelled sweaters, Gordie Howe was a sports adviser to Eaton's, Bobby Hull promoted hockey skates (by Bauer) and gloves (by Winnwell), Johnny Bower was used in ads by Elmer's Glue and Andy Bathgate told of the pleasures of living in Bramalea, Ontario.

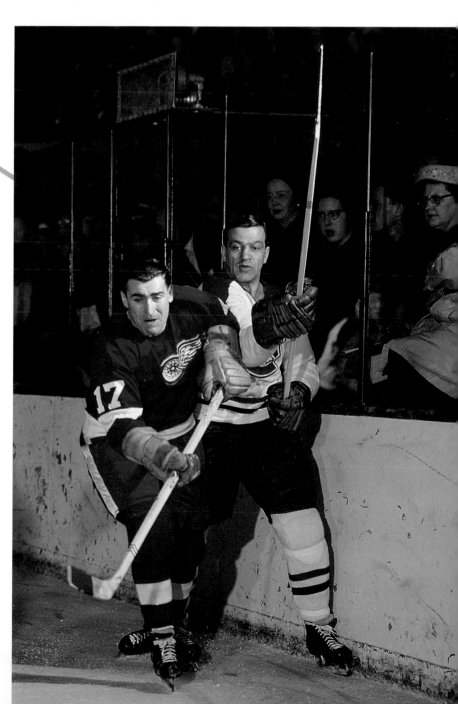

BILL GADSBY

Bill Gadsby (#4) of the Red Wings keeps a close eye on Leafs player Red Kelly. Gadsby began his 20-year NHL career with Chicago before being dealt to the New York Rangers. Detroit picked him up in a 1961 deal, and he became the second player in league history (Gordie Howe was the first) to play in 1,000 career games. Going to Detroit gave Gadsby three chances to win a Stanley Cup (1963, 1964, 1966), but the Red Wings could not pull out a victory in the finals. He played in 1,248 games, scoring 130 goals and 567 points.

Leonard "Red" Kelly was on eight Stanley Cup-winning teams (four in Detroit, four in Toronto) and is tied with Henri Richard for most games played in the finals (65). In all, Kelly made 12 appearances in the finals, tying him for the record with Maurice Richard, Henri Richard and Jean Béliveau. In addition to playing hockey, Kelly was a member of Parliament (York West riding in Toronto), winning a seat in two federal elections in the mid-sixties.

"As time goes along, you'll be seeing more players wearing helmets in the NHL."

— *Red Kelly* (Hockey Illustrated, *April 1965*)

Kelly decided to wear a helmet after suffering a couple of concussions in 1962-63. The helmet he wore was made in Sweden and cost $5 to $6. Kelly took the helmet off in 1966-67, his last season in the NHL. When Bill Masterton died of head injuries sustained in an NHL game on January 15, 1968, his wife received $50,000 from life insurance coverage.

UNUSUAL NOTE

Red Kelly and his wife, Andra, sent thank you notes to members of the Toronto media for making him and his family feel welcome after his February 1960 trade to Toronto (the Leafs had sent Marc Reaume to Detroit).

Of the top five players who have won the most Stanley Cups, Red Kelly is the only one not to have played for the Montreal Canadiens. The others: Henri Richard, 11 Stanley Cups; Jean Béliveau, 10; Yvan Cournoyer, 10; Claude Provost, 9; Maurice Richard, 8; Red Kelly, 8; Jacques Lemaire, 8

STATS

HARRY HOWELL

New York's Harry Howell (#3) goes down to block a shot against a swarm of Blackhawks, including Bobby Hull (#9) and Johnny Mckenzie (#18). Howell began his NHL career with the Rangers in 1952 right from their junior team in Guelph, Ontario. He scored his first goal in his first NHL game at Toronto by beating Leafs goalie Harry Lumley in a 4-3 Ranger loss on October 18, 1952. Not overly aggressive, Howell's style occaisionally earned him the wrath of Rangers fans, but he stayed in New York until 1969. He became the first Ranger to play in 1,000 games, and he was honoured for the achievement with a special night on January 25, 1967, when he received $7,500 in gifts, including a new Mercury Cougar car. (Howell's salary in 1966 was reported to have been $16,000.) The 1966-67 season was his finest; he scored a career high 12 goals and 40 points, gaining a first-team all-star berth and his only Norris Trophy (the last to win it before Bobby Orr's streak of eight in a row). After stops in Oakland and Los Angeles, Howell finished his career with 1,411 games played. He was elected to the Hall of Fame in 1979.

BROTHER ACT

Harry Howell's brother, Ron, was also a good athlete and played in four NHL games with New York between 1954 and 1956 (no goals, no assists). Ron was better known as a football player in the CFL (Toronto, Montreal, Hamilton), and he played minor league hockey when football season was over. Howell's brother-in-law was fellow NHLer and one-time teammate Ron Murphy.

UNUSUAL NOTE

WOR-TV, the local New York CBS affiliate, was showing the Chicago-Detroit game on Sunday afternoon, February 12, 1967, "live and in colour." With 11 minutes to go, the broadcast was abruptly dropped to show the Addams Family sitcom. To explain the mistake, the station said that it was used to taped two-hour broadcasts of Rangers contests and was unprepared for the live CBS game, which ran late. The fans watching did not miss any goals in the 3-2 Chicago win.

DAVE KEON

"You can't help the team when you're in the penalty box. The important thing is that you can accomplish anything in hockey without getting penalized."

— *Dave Keon* (Hockey Pictorial, *March 1966*)

Marketing the Game

Prior to the start of the 1963-64 season, the Maple Leafs played in 17 exhibition games. Only seven of the games were against NHL teams, whereas seven were played versus WHL teams (including one against the Western League all-stars) and three were played against AHL clubs. Prior to the start of the 1997-98 season, all the Leafs 10 preseason games were played against NHL competition.

Dave Keon (#14) surprised the Maple Leafs by making the team as a 20-year-old rookie in 1960-61. He played his way onto the team with an outstanding exhibition season (the Leafs toured the West Coast), and he scored his first NHL goal on October 9, 1960, in a 3-3 tie at the Detroit Olympia against the Red Wings. The lightning-quick centre scored 20 goals as a rookie and won the Calder Trophy, his first major award. A gentlemanly player throughout his career, Keon won the Lady Byng Trophy twice and added the Conn Smythe to his silverware collection for his performance in the 1967 playoffs. Keon considered Joe DiMaggio of the New York Yankees as the ideal role model, and the future Leafs captain himself became a hero to many youngsters who followed the Leafs in the sixties. He became so valuable to the Maple Leafs that coach Punch Imlach once declared, "I wouldn't take a million dollars for Keon" (*Hockey Illustrated*, December 1963).

STATS

Dave Keon was always at his best during the playoffs, with his greatest performance coming in the seventh game of the 1964 semifinals versus Montreal, when he scored all three goals in a 3-1 Toronto win (a game he dedicated to his sick father). He also shone brightly on April 18, 1963, when he scored two shorthanded goals in one playoff game (the first NHL player to do so) as the Leafs captured the Stanley Cup with a 3-1 victory over Detroit. Keon once held the Leafs record for most career playoff goals with 32 (until it was broken by Wendel Clark in 1996), and his 67 points (in 84 games) were only surpassed recently by Doug Gilmour (who had 77 points in 52 games).

CLAUDE PROVOST

"Provost gets a lot of scoring opportunities because he checks, and when a player checks he winds up with the puck. It's a wonder more players don't realize that."

Toe Blake (Hockey News, *February 10, 1968*)

"He's a nuisance to me but I respect him."

Bobby Hull on Claude Provost (Hockey News, *August 1968*)

Marketing the Game

Collecting player trading cards began to develop during the fifties and continued to have a prominent role during the sixties in marketing the game of hockey. One of the most notable sets was produced by the Topps Gum Company for the 1964-65 issue, which became known as "tallboys" because the cards were more than four and a half inches tall. The 110-card set was the first to include all six NHL teams.

Canadiens player Claude Provost (#14), on the far right, checks Leafs player Eddie Shack (#23) behind the net. Provost joined the Montreal team in 1955-56, just in time for the first of five straight Stanley Cups. Primarily a defensive forward, Provost had a career high 33 goals in 1961-62 and gained a first-team all-star berth on right wing after the 1964-65 season, when he had 27 tallies and 64 points. Provost then added eight points in 13 playoff games as Montreal reclaimed the Stanley Cup in 1965. Provost had scored an overtime winner to eliminate defending champion Toronto and then shut down Chicago's Bobby Hull with a superior checking effort (Hull's only two goals came when Provost was not on the ice.) In 1967-68 Provost was the first recipient of the Masterton Trophy, edging out Ed Westfall and Ron Ellis for the award.

AB McDONALD

Chicago's Ab McDonald (#14) cuts across the crease of Montreal goalie Jacques Plante. The Blackhawks acquired the big left winger in a cash deal in June 1960 after he had spent three seasons with the Canadiens (including three Stanley Cups in 1958, 1959 and 1960). McDonald scored 17 goals in 1960-61 and added four playoff points in helping Chicago to a Cup win, scoring the clinching goal in the process. He became best known as a member of the "Scooter Line" (along with Stan Mikita and Ken Wharram) and played in Chicago until the end of the 1963-64 season. McDonald was dealt to Boston along with Reggie Fleming for Doug Mohns and later played for Detroit, Pittsburgh (he was the first captain there) and St. Louis (where he scored a career high 25 goals).

The Money Game

When Jacques Plante was traded to the New York Rangers for the 1963-64 season, he signed a contract for $25,000 US (worth $27,000 Canadian at the time). NHL teams paid their players in the currency of the country in which they played. The pension contribution of $900 paid by the players was in Canadian dollars for everyone.

UNUSUAL NOTE

Jacques Plante once made the following suggestions to improve the game: two referees (now used on an experimental basis in the pre-season), larger goal creases (implemented to protect goalies), ejection of players who get five-minute majors (implemented in certain situations, such as hitting from behind), an award for the best goalie (which the Vezina Trophy has recognized since 1982) and goalie coaches (which most teams now have).

DOUG BARKLEY

Detroit's Doug Barkley (#5) moves in to check Toronto's Jim Pappin (#18). The Red Wings gave up two forwards (Len Lunde and Johnny McKenzie) to Chicago to acquire the big defenceman from Lethbridge, Alberta. Finally getting a chance to play in the NHL at 26 years old, Barkley responded with three goals and 24 assists in 1962-63 to finish second in the Calder Trophy voting. He followed up with 11 goals and 32 points in 1963-64 while racking up 115 penalty minutes and helping the Red Wings to their second consecutive appearance in the finals. Just as Barkley was reaching his prime, a stick in the eye 43 games into the 1965-66 season ended his career. He received $20,000 under the NHL's insurance plan for the loss of sight in his right eye. Barkley finished with 104 points in 253 games.

Jim Pappin was an excellent goal scorer in the minors (seasons of 28, 34 and 36 goals) but had difficulty cracking the Toronto line-up. He was with the Leafs in 1964 when they beat Detroit for the Stanley Cup, but his best moment came in 1967 when he led all playoff scoring with 15 points and scored the winning goal in the last game against Montreal.

"I'd sooner be farmed out in the Leaf organization than play elsewhere in the NHL. I know I'll get another chance if I play well in Rochester."

– *Jim Pappin* (Hockey World, *January 1968*)

UNUSUAL NOTE

By 1964-65 all NHL teams were travelling by airplane (the Red Wings had been the first team to start flying, in 1958-59) almost exclusively. Most teams had 20 to 30 trips scheduled by air (the Leafs had 30), except for Montreal, which had only 16 airplane trips booked for the season. Because of the increased air travel, the NHL took out a $2-million policy ($100,000 per person for 20 players) for each team in the event of a disaster. A number of NHL players—including Bob Nevin, Lou Fontinato, Billy Harris and Don Marshall—married stewardesses.

The Money Game

Executives of the Maple Leafs put pressure on general manager Punch Imlach in 1964-65 because the team had too many players earning an NHL salary and not playing regularly in Toronto (Don McKenney, Jim Pappin) or in the minors (Ed Litzenberger, Larry Hillman, Al Arbour, Bronco Horvath). All these players were moved out over a three-year period. From 1995 to 1997, Maple Leafs executives ordered general manager Cliff Fletcher to reduce an unproductively high payroll, forcing the trading of Dave Andreychuk, Mike Gartner, Dave Gagner, Todd Gill and Larry Murphy.

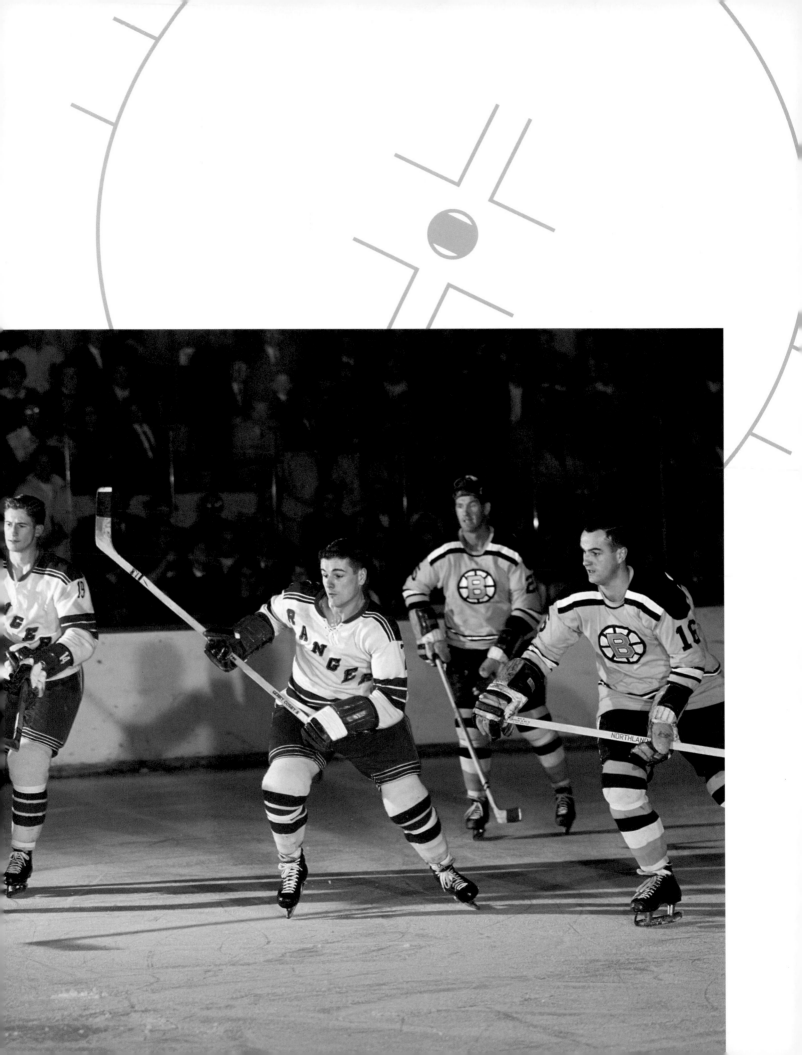

ROD GILBERT

Rangers forward Rod Gilbert (#7) tries to get away from the checking of the Bruins Murray Oliver (#16). Gilbert earned an assist on a Dean Prentice goal in his first NHL game as the Rangers and the Blackhawks tied 3-3 on November 28, 1960. He scored his first goal in the playoffs when New York faced Toronto on April 3, 1962, by picking off an Allan Stanley pass and putting a shot past Johnny Bower. He then scored two goals and three assists during that year's playoff series versus the Leafs. In 1963-64 Gilbert scored 24 goals and had 64 points in only his second full NHL season. His greatest game was on February 28, 1968, when he beat Canadiens netminder Rogie Vachon four times (on 16 shots) in a 6-1 New York win at the Montreal Forum. (Gilbert once scored five goals in one game as a junior.) Gilbert's career was nearly cut short by a serious back injury, but he went on to hold the Rangers all-time records for goals (406), assists (615) and points (1,021). He won the Masterton Trophy in 1975.

"I've been with the Rangers for three years and my ambition is to play for 20 years in the NHL and to score 400 goals. I'd like to do it all with New York."
– Rod Gilbert (Hockey Illustrated, *January 1966*)

"Sure I go out a lot. It's my way of relaxing. Some guys like to sleep. I like to chase girls."
– Rod Gilbert (Hockey News, *March 23, 1968*)

The Money Game

In 1967-68 Rod Gilbert was the highest-paid Ranger, earning $36,000 per season. In 1997-98 Wayne Gretzky had the highest salary on the Rangers, earning $6.5 million a year.

BOBBY BAUN

Toronto's Bobby Baun (#21) blocks the path of Detroit's Ron Murphy (#12). During the 1963-64 season, Baun missed 18 games with a broken finger, but at playoff time he didn't let a broken leg stop him. On April 23, 1964, the Leafs desperately needed to beat the Red Wings in the sixth game of the finals at the Olympia to retain a chance at three straight Stanley Cups. Injured by blocking a shot and removed on a stretcher in the third period, Baun returned to action late in the game (the score was tied 3-3), and he joined his mates for the overtime session. His ankle had been shot with painkiller and was taped tightly so that he could put his skate back on. At 1:43 of overtime, he let a shot go from the point that deflected off the stick of Detroit defenceman Bill Gadsby and sailed over the shoulder of Terry Sawchuk for the game winner. Baun played the next game, and the Leafs shut out the Red Wings 4-0 to complete their Stanley Cup hat trick. Ironically, Baun played in all 70 games in 1964-65 and did not score a single goal in the season or the playoffs! He finished his career with 37 goals and 224 points.

UNUSUAL NOTE

The Leafs Bob Pulford got the only assist on Bobby Baun's famous broken-leg goal against Detroit, and he wasn't even on the ice! Dave Keon, Billy Harris, George Armstrong and Carl Brewer were on the ice with Baun when the goal was scored. It's likely that the referee meant to give the assist to Brewer (#2), who had shot the puck into the Red Wings end, and not to Pulford (#20).

TRIVIA

When Ron Murphy played for the Boston Bruins in 1967-68, he wore the highest sweater number, 28, for any player other than a goalie. Frank Mahovlich of the Leafs was next with number 27. Prior to the start of the 1997-98 season, Ottawa Senators general manager Pierre Gauthier declared that no player on his team would wear a sweater with a number higher than 35. Gauthier believes that high numbers (now common in the NHL) make the player stand out from his teammates and that the practice hurts the team concept.

HENRI RICHARD

Montreal's Henri Richard (#16) tries to escape the clutches of Toronto's Carl Brewer (#2). The Canadiens centre had a tough act to follow being the brother of the great Maurice "Rocket" Richard, but the "Pocket Rocket" proved he was a star in his own right. He scored his first NHL goal in his fourth game, on October 15, 1955, beating Rangers goalie Gump Worsley after receiving passes from Jean-Guy Talbot and Bert Olmstead in a 4-1 Canadiens victory at the Forum. He won a Stanley Cup in his first five years in the league (contributing 35 points in 41 games) and 11 championships in total before his 20-season career ended in 1975. His best-remembered goals were two Stanley Cup winners (1966 versus Detroit's Roger Crozier and 1971 against Chicago's Tony Esposito), and the Hall of Famer finished with 358 goals and 1,046 points.

A rugged rearguard, Carl Brewer was an outstanding skater who played the game on the edge. A three-time all-star, he anchored a Leafs defence that won three Cups in a row before he left the team in 1965. He was out of the NHL until 1969 but returned to play for the Detroit Red Wings, who reportedly gave him a $50,000 contract (he once held out from the Leafs camp over $100) and reunited him with former partner Bobby Baun.

"When you add everything up about Richard, the thing to remember about him is that he's a clutch player. He gets a goal when you need it most."
— *Toe Blake* (Hockey Illustrated, *April-May 1967*)

The Money Game

For winning the Stanley Cup in 1969, Henri Richard and his Canadien teammates each received $3,000. Their opponents, the St. Louis Blues, each got $1,500. Finishing first in the East or West Division (which both Montreal and St. Louis did in 1968-69) was worth $2,250 per player.

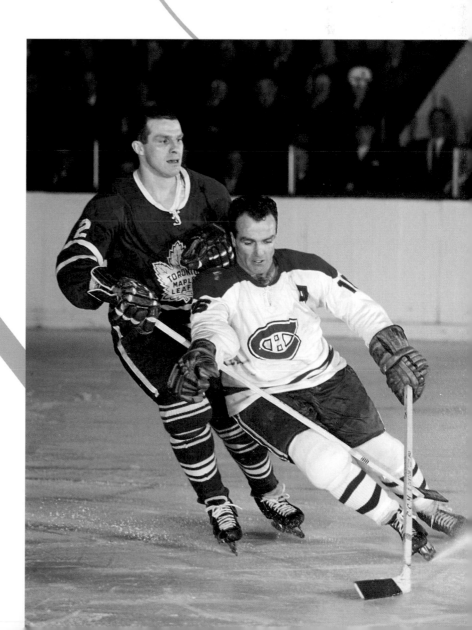

PIERRE PILOTE

Chicago's Pierre Pilote (#3) has his eye on Toronto's George Armstrong (#10) in front of goalie Glenn Hall. The 1963-64 season saw Pilote win the second of his three consecutive Norris Trophies as the NHL's best defenceman. He had seven goals and 46 assists for the Blackhawks and was one of five Chicago players to make the first all-star team for that season (Hall, Hull, Mikita and Wharram were the others.) Pilote edged Toronto's Tim Horton (his partner on the first all-star team) for the Norris. Small but rugged, Pilote led the league in penalty minutes (165) in 1960-61. An excellent point man, he totalled 80 career goals to go with 498 points. Pilote's last season was with Toronto in 1968-69.

Marketing the Game

In 1964-65 the Coca-Cola Company offered drinkers of Coke and Sprite a head shot on the bottle cap featuring players from all six NHL teams. The soft drink makers also offered an ice rink-shaped plaque (with team logos) on which to mount the caps. The plaque cost 75 cents and held 108 caps. Special cork liners offered $5 prizes or tickets to the Stanley Cup playoffs.

Trivia

Pierre Pilote is one of only three Blackhawks to win the Norris Trophy. The others are Doug Wilson (1982) and Chris Chelios (1993, 1996).

ALEX DELVECCHIO

The father of Detroit's Alex Delvecchio (#10) wanted his son to become an engineer, but the young hockey player was too talented not to pursue a career in the game. An outstanding junior in Oshawa, Delvecchio played in only six minor league games before joining the Red Wings in 1951-52, recording 15 goals and 37 points as a rookie and winning his first Stanley Cup. He won three Cups with Detroit in the fifties, and he only got better in the sixties, when he scored 216 goals between 1960-61 and 1968-69. A three-time Lady Byng winner, Delvecchio also captained the Red Wings from 1962 to 1973. His coach, Sid Abel, once said of him, "He is perhaps the best captain the Wings ever had. When he says something the players listen. He doesn't get excited and everyone respects him" (*Hockey Illustrated*, February 1968). Delvecchio's career spanned 24 seasons, ending in 1973-74 after 1,549 games, 456 goals and 1,281 points. His sweater number, 10, has been retired by the Red Wings, along with Gordie Howe's #9, Ted Lindsay's #7, Sid Abel's #12, Terry Sawchuk's #1 and Larry Aurie's #6.

"Expansion is going to dilute the talent in the league and it should add two or three seasons to careers for guys like myself and Howe."

– *Alex Delvecchio* (Hockey Illustrated, *January 1966*)

MILESTONE GOAL

Alex Delvecchio scored his 300th career goal (only the ninth NHL player to do so at the time) on February 3, 1966, against the Boston Bruins and goalie Bernie Parent. Only four other players have scored 300 or more goals as a Red Wing: Gordie Howe (786), Ted Lindsay (335), Norm Ullman (324) and Steve Yzerman (563 and still active).

When the Maple Leafs were whipped 11-0 by Boston on home ice, they recorded only 20 bodychecks in that game. The next game they had 70 hits in Chicago and won 2-0.

DEAN PRENTICE

Boston's Dean Prentice (#17) is about to score on Toronto goaltender Don Simmons (#24). Prentice played in 22 NHL seasons and in 1,378 games (10th all-time highest total). He spent over 10 seasons with the New York Rangers before being traded to Boston for Don McKenney in 1963. The 1963-64 season was his first full year with the Bruins, and Prentice scored 23 goals in 70 games. He had 10 seasons with 20 or more goals. After his stay in Boston, Prentice moved on to Detroit, Pittsburgh and Minnesota. His career totals include 391 goals and 860 points. Along with Doug Mohns, Harry Howell and Norm Ullman, Prentice is one of four players to be on the top-10 list of all-time games played and not to have won a Stanley Cup.

Overshadowed playing behind future Hall Of Famers, Don Simmons was typical of the "unsung heroes," the back-up goaltenders during the Original Six era. Simmons broke into the league with Boston in the 1956-57 season and played 11 seasons with the Bruins, Leafs and Rangers. Though never a household name, he racked up 98 wins and 39 ties in 247 career games, with 20 shutouts and a goals-against average of 2.93 (2.67 in 24 playoff games).

Unusual Note

After losing 11-0 to Boston on January 18, 1964, Toronto played in Chicago the following night. Maple Leafs coach Punch Imlach did not want to use goalie Don Simmons after watching him get bombed by the Bruins. Toronto's regular goaltender, Johnny Bower, was out with an injury, as was Gerry Cheevers, the top goalie in the Leafs farm system. Imlach elected to call up Al Millar from Denver of the WHL; he was playing well and had some NHL experience. But Millar's plane was unable to land at O'Hare Airport and then experienced mechanical problems in Des Moines, Iowa. Simmons was forced back into the net, and he shut out the league-leading Blackhawks 2-0 on goals by Ron Stewart and Billy Harris. Millar never played in the NHL again, whereas Simmons left Toronto at the end of the season to finish his career with the Rangers.

TRIVIA

On January 8, 1967, Dean Prentice, with Detroit at the time, scored his 250th career goal. It gave the Red Wings a total of five players on their 1966-67 team who had scored 250 or more career goals. The others were Gordie Howe, Andy Bathgate, Alex Delvecchio and Norm Ullman.

35

KENT DOUGLAS

Kent Douglas was the first defenceman to win the Calder Trophy, and since that time there have been seven other blueliners to win the coveted award: Jacques Laperriere (Montreal, 1964), Bobby Orr (Boston, 1967), Denis Potvin (New York Islanders, 1974), Ray Bourque (Boston, 1980), Gary Suter (Calgary, 1986), Brian Leetch (New York Rangers, 1989) and Bryan Berard (New York Islanders, 1997).

The Money Game

The Maple Leafs started showing their road games at movie theatres in the early sixties. In the first year, they sold 92 percent of the seats available at the one theatre showing the games. By 1963-64 they had spread the idea to nine theatres (six in Toronto and one each in Hamilton, Oshawa and St. Catharines).

Toronto's Kent Douglas (#19) fires the puck away from Detroit's Norm Ullman (#7). The Leafs gave up five players to the Springfield Indians (AHL) to acquire Douglas after he had won the Eddie Shore Award as the best defenceman in the AHL. He joined the Leafs for the 1962-63 season and won the Calder Trophy as a 27-year-old rookie (edging out another rearguard, Doug Barkley of Detroit.) Douglas played 70 games that season, scoring seven goals and 15 assists and recording 105 penalty minutes. He also helped Toronto to a second straight Stanley Cup, assisting on the clinching goal by Eddie Shack. An aggressive player, he was also known for wearing charcoal under his eyes to fight the glare of the television lights. He stayed with Toronto until 1967-68, when he was drafted by the Oakland Seals. He went on to play for Detroit and finished with 33 goals and 115 assists in 428 career games.

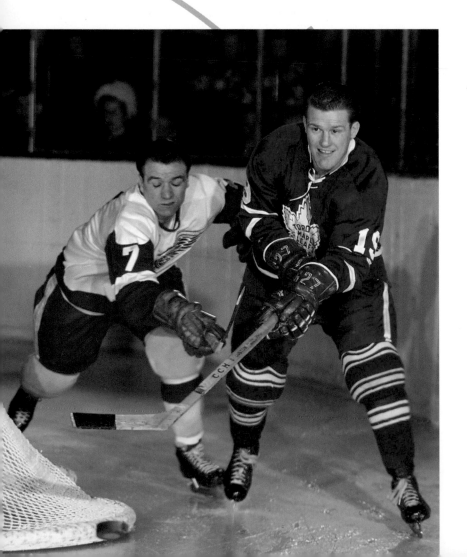

CHARLIE HODGE

Canadiens goalie Charlie Hodge (#1) reaches for a loose puck while Henri Richard (#16) and Terry Harper (#19) look to help out. The 1963-64 season was a breakthrough for the Montreal netminder. After many years as the backup for the Canadiens (primarily spent in the minor leagues), Hodge was given the opportunity when Jacques Plante was traded. Hodge responded with a league high of eight shutouts and 33 victories, winning the Vezina Trophy with a 2.26 goals-against average. The Canadiens finished in first place but were knocked off in the playoffs by Toronto. Hodge shared a Vezina Trophy with Gump Worsley in 1965-66 and was selected in both expansion drafts of 1967 (Oakland) and 1970 (Vancouver).

"I think a goalie would feel much better if he could sit up in the stands with his regular clothes on and then rush down and change when needed [rather than sit on the bench]. After all, how often is a goalie called into action this way?"

– *Charlie Hodge* (Hockey Pictorial, *December 1965*)

The NHL passed a rule for the 1965-66 season that each team must dress a backup goalie.

Unusual Note

Of the 17 regular Montreal Canadiens in 1963-64, nine were French and eight were English. Two came from Montreal, eight from other parts of Quebec, two from Ontario, four from Saskatchewan and one from British Columbia. Charlie Hodge was the only bilingual English player on the team. Of the 30 players who helped Montreal to win the Stanley Cup in 1993, 14 were born in Quebec.

NORM ULLMAN

Red Wings centre Norm Ullman (#7) had seven straight years of 20 or more goals prior to 1964-65, when he had a league-leading 42 goals. He had 10 game-winning goals that year and assisted on 10 more game winners, giving him a major hand in 20 of 40 Detroit wins. His performance gained him his only first all-star team selection. Ullman was edged out by Bobby Hull for the Hart Trophy, and his salary for the following season (1965-66) was a reported $20,000. One of the NHL's top forecheckers, Ullman played 13 seasons for Detroit (875 games, 324 goals, 758 points) before he was dealt to Toronto in 1968. He had 35 goals for the Leafs in 1970-71 and ended his NHL career after 1974-75. Ullman served as the second president of the NHL Players' Association.

"The trouble in the past was that players were so anxious to become pro hockey players they'd play for nothing. Now they're realizing there are other things in life and that they have rights."

– *Alan Eagleson* (Hockey News, *March 4, 1967*)

The Money Game

In 1961-62 a Detroit Red Wings sweater could be purchased for $3.95, and a game program cost 25 cents. In the 1966 exhibition game season, the Red Wings experimented with player names on the backs of the jerseys. In 1967-68 the Red Wings signed a three-year deal with Stroh's Brewery for $500,000 for radio (all 74 games) and television (31 road games) rights.

MILESTONE GOAL

Norm Ullman scored his 100th career goal against the Boston Bruins on November 3, 1960, in an 8-5 Detroit win. The Red Wings trailed the Bruins 5-2 at the Detroit Olympia, but two goals by Ullman helped to spark a comeback.

BRIT SELBY

Toronto's Brit Selby (#11) takes a shot at Chicago goaltender Dave Dryden (#30). Selby joined the Leafs after a stellar junior career with the Toronto Marlboros. He scored his first NHL goal (during a three-game call-up in 1964-65) against Rangers netminder Jacques Plante on January 3, 1965, in a 3-3 tie, with the assists going to Carl Brewer and Kent Douglas. Selby scored 14 goals as a rookie in 1965-66 and won the Calder Trophy. His rising star quickly fell back to Earth (assisted by a broken leg), and he only played in six games in 1966-67 for the Leafs. He went to Philadelphia in the expansion draft and had 15 goals for the Flyers in 1967-68 before returning to Toronto the following season. He also played for St. Louis and totalled 55 goals and 62 assists in his NHL career.

"They protected Allan Stanley and he's 42 years old. I'm only 22. To be truthful I'm glad to get out of the Maple Leafs organization. I certainly feel I'm better off playing on a younger club."

– *Brit Selby* (Hockey News, *October 14, 1967*)

UNUSUAL NOTE

Goaltender Dave Dryden played his first NHL game as a New York Ranger on February 3, 1962, when — as the "house goalie" at Maple Leaf Gardens (watching the game in the stands) — he replaced the injured Gump Worsley. He allowed three Toronto goals in a 4-1 loss, although he did make 23 saves. It was the only game he played in 1961-62, earning $100 for his efforts.

TRIVIA

Brit Selby made the 1964-65 Ontario Hockey Association (OHA) first all-star team as a left winger (45 goals, 43 assists). Other future NHL players on the team were Bernie Parent (goal), Jim McKenney and Gilles Marotte (tied for one defence spot), Bobby Orr (defence), André Lacroix (centre) and Ken Hodge (right wing).

BOB NEVIN

Rangers Bob Nevin (#8) discusses matters with the officials before all the sticks and gloves are picked up after a brawl with the Leafs. Nevin made his debut in the NHL as a Maple Leaf in 1960-61, when he scored 21 goals and 37 assists, finishing second to teammate Dave Keon for the Calder Trophy as best rookie. He played on two Stanley Cup teams for the Leafs (1962, 1963) before slumping in the 1963-64 season. Toronto general manager Punch Imlach sent Nevin and Dick Duff to New York, and by 1965-66 Nevin had regained his scoring touch with 29 markers and 62 points. He took over as captain of the Rangers on February 5, 1965, and stayed in that role until the end of the 1970-71 season. Nevin's best seasons in New York came when he played on a line with Phil Goyette and Don Marshall, including a career high 31 goals in 1968-69. He went to the Minnesota North Stars and then to the Los Angeles Kings (where he also scored 31 goals one season). He played until 1975-76 and has totals of 307 goals and 726 points in 1,128 games.

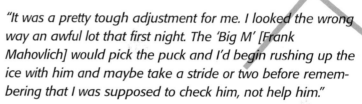

"It was a pretty tough adjustment for me. I looked the wrong way an awful lot that first night. The 'Big M' [Frank Mahovlich] would pick the puck and I'd begin rushing up the ice with him and maybe take a stride or two before remembering that I was supposed to check him, not help him."

— Bob Nevin on the night he was traded from the Leafs to the Rangers and then had to go out and face his former teammates (after he had taken the morning skate with Toronto) on February 22, 1964. The Leafs won the game 5-2. (Hockey Illustrated, *February 1968*)

UNUSUAL NOTE

New York coach and general manager Emile "the Cat" Francis got into a brawl with fans at Madison Square Garden on November 21, 1965, when he went to protest to the goal judge about a goal scored by the visiting Detroit Red Wings. Some of the New York fans turned on Francis, and Rangers forward Vic Hadfield scaled the tall glass behind the net to rescue the coach. Other Rangers to scale the glass included Arnie Brown, Earl Ingerfield, Reg Fleming and Mike McMahon. As many as 10 Rangers joined in the melee with the fans, but the goal stood and the game ended in a 3-3 tie.

GLENN HALL

Chicago goalie Glenn Hall (#1) battles Detroit's Parker MacDonald (#20) for a loose puck. Although he put up impressive numbers in Detroit, the Red Wings dealt Hall to the Blackhawks in 1957, where he won his first Vezina Trophy, in 1962-63 (five shutouts and a 2.54 goals-against average in 66 games). He continued a streak of consecutive games played with the Blackhawks (502 in total), and he was honoured for the achievement one night by being given a station wagon. Montreal then promptly beat him for seven goals! He took the Blackhawks to the Cup in 1961 by playing in all 12 playoff games, recording two shutouts along the way. Hall shared a second Vezina with Denis DeJordy in 1966-67, his last with Chicago. He moved to St. Louis in the expansion draft (where he was given a $47,500 contract) and won the Conn Smythe Trophy for his 1968 playoff performance, which took the Blues to the finals. He shared another Vezina Trophy with Jacques Plante in 1968-69 and stayed with the Blues until 1970-71.

"I owe everything to hockey. It truly is a tremendous game. But professional hockey is a business and although I don't enjoy playing it anymore, it's a business I can't afford to get out of yet."

— *Glenn Hall* (Hockey Pictorial, *November 1967*)

UNUSUAL NOTE

During the sixties, Parker MacDonald — a native of Sydney, Nova Scotia — was one of the few players in the NHL born in the Maritime provinces of Canada. Other Maritimers included Willie O'Ree (Fredericton, NB), Gerry Ouellette (Grand Falls, NB), Forbes Kennedy (Dorchester, NB), Al MacNeil (New Glasgow, NS) and Alex Faulkner (Bishops Falls, NF).

CESARE MANIAGO

One of the tallest goalies of his era (six foot three inches), Cesare Maniago started his NHL career in 1960-61 with the Maple Leafs by playing in seven games. One of those games saw Maniago give up Bernie Geoffrion's 50th goal of the season at the Montreal Forum. For the next six years, he mostly played in the minors (except for 14 games with the Canadiens in 1962-63) before finally becoming a regular with the New York Rangers in 1965-66, when he played in 27 games. Maniago gave up Bobby Hull's 51st goal of the season, but he did record two shutouts. He was the first player taken by the Minnesota North Stars in the expansion draft and played in 48 games for them in 1967-68, notching six shutouts and a respectable 2.77 goals-against average. Three of the six shutouts were recorded consecutively (he was the first goalie to do so since Glenn Hall in 1955-56 with Detroit) and included 4-0 and 3-0 wins over the Los Angeles Kings and a 1-0 victory over Oakland. Maniago moved on to play for Vancouver and finished his career with 189 wins, 96 ties and 30 shutouts in 568 games played.

"Expansion has been tremendous for me. I'd be second string with New York behind Eddie [Giacomin]. There'd be no way I'd get raises. This way I've got another four or five years at a pretty good salary."

– *Cesare Maniago* (Hockey Illustrated, *January 1970*)

UNUSUAL NOTE

Emil Otto "Pop" Kenesky started making the modern goalie pads in 1924 within his family business, which went by the name of Barton Sports and Cycle Company. The standard pad that Kenesky made by hand was 28 inches tall originally, but by 1964 the height of the pads had gone as high as 31 or 32 inches. The width of the pad was reduced from 12 to 10 inches (it was put back to 12 in 1989-90), and the weight was about 11 pounds. These custom-made pads sold for $83.50 in 1964.

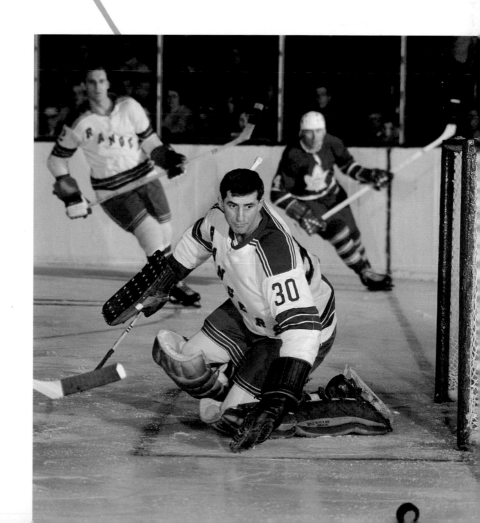

BERNIE PARENT

Boston goaltender Bernie Parent (#30) watches the action behind the net as New York's Vic Hadfield (#11) tries to muscle Bruins defenceman Don Awrey (#26). Parent began his NHL career with the Bruins in 1965-66, recording a 2-2 tie in his first game, against Chicago. After an 8-1 loss to the Red Wings, Parent won his first game at the Montreal Forum in a 3-1 Bruins victory. He gained his first career shutout in a 2-0 win over the Maple Leafs. The Bruins were high on this young goalie and paid $3,000 to get him to their junior team in Niagara Falls. However, he was left unprotected in the expansion draft and was quickly snapped up by the Philadelphia Flyers. As a Flyer, Parent won two Vezina Trophies and a pair of Stanley Cups (1974 and 1975).

Don Awrey was a strong skater who played an aggressive game at the blueline. He once tied an NHL record with 37 penalty minutes in one game versus the Montreal Canadiens on December 3, 1967, in a 5-3 Boston win. Awrey had one minor, three majors, one misconduct and one game misconduct in the contest. He was a member of Team Canada in 1972.

"I've always wanted to be a hockey player. I have an older brother who went on to the University of Toronto but I wasn't that dedicated with the books, so I knew either I have to make it as a hockey player or buy a lunch bucket."
— *Don Awrey* (Hockey News, *January 2, 1965*)

TRIVIA

Plucked from the Chicago organization, Vic Hadfield became a much sought after player when he led the NHL in penalty minutes with 151 in 1963-64 with the Rangers. As his career progressed, he proved to be more than just a tough guy. In 1971-72 he became the first Ranger to score 50 goals in a season (Adam Graves has been the only other Ranger to hit the 50-goal mark; he had 52 in 1993-94). Hadfield scored 262 career goals and 572 points for New York and was team captain before being dealt to Pittsburgh. He was a member of Team Canada in 1972.

UNUSUAL NOTE

A native of Montreal, Bernie Parent lived next door to the sister of goaltending legend Jacques Plante. When Plante visited his sister, Parent would go over and get tips from the Vezina Trophy winner. Parent learned his lessons well and became a teammate of Plante when they were both with the Maple Leafs in 1971 and 1972. Parent has often credited Plante's advice as one reason he became a successful goaltender.

45

JEAN BÉLIVEAU

Montreal's Jean Béliveau (#4) battles for the puck with Toronto's Red Kelly (wearing helmet) and Tim Horton. Béliveau won his second Hart Trophy as the NHL's most valuable player in 1963-64 (28 goals and 78 points), and he was named the first recipient of the Conn Smythe Trophy for his performance in the 1965 playoffs. In 13 games, Béliveau had 16 points (8 goals, 8 assists) and scored the quickest Stanley Cup-winning goal just 14 seconds into the seventh game versus the Blackhawks. For winning the Smythe, Béliveau received $1,000 from the league, and that amount was matched by the Canadiens. (In 1997 Detroit Red Wings goalie Mike Vernon received $10,000 from the NHL as the Smythe winner.) The championship also marked the first time Béliveau accepted the Cup as captain of the team, something he would do five times in total. A 10-time Cup winner, he scored 79 playoff goals and 176 points (still Montreal club records) in 162 games. His playoff point total makes Béliveau the only player from the "original six" era to rank in the top-10 list of the all-time playoff scorers. By the end of the sixties, Béliveau was reportedly earning about $55,000 a year (in 1969-70).

Marketing the Game

In 1961-62 the Montreal Canadiens yearbook sold for 55 cents. Included in the price were a set of postcard photos and an 8" x 10" colour team photo. The Stanley Cup-champion Maple Leafs sold their 1962-63 yearbook for 60 cents, and the Red Wings sold theirs for $1 the same season.

UNUSUAL NOTE

Punch Imlach took his team to Los Angeles for a game early in the 1968-69 season only to find the Forum ice covered with a basketball court when he wanted the Leafs to practice. Not one to waste an opportunity, Imlach chose sides and made his team play basketball. "They needed the exercise," he said. He kept four players out for extra shooting practice because "they weren't hustling"

(Hockey News, *December 21, 1968*).

The Money Game

One of the most successful coaches in hockey during the sixties (four Stanley Cups and 39 playoff victories), Punch Imlach was never easy on his players. He became even more demanding after expansion and told all the Leafs that they would be fined $100 for any loss to an expansion team. The Maple Leafs lost 11 games to the new teams in 1967-68.

EDDIE SHACK

It wasn't often that Leafs coach Punch Imlach saw eye to eye with winger Eddie Shack. A big, strong skater with a good but inaccurate shot, Shack rarely got regular ice time under Imlach, although he did score the Stanley Cup-winning goal in 1963 against Detroit and potted 26 markers for Toronto in 1965-66. "The Entertainer," as Shack was known, liked to play an aggressive game that sometimes got out of control. He was once jailed while with the New York Rangers when he got into a stick-swinging incident with Hershey's Eddie Mazur during an exhibition game in Niagara Falls. As a Bruin, he also had a celebrated stick duel with Philadelphia's Larry Zeidel in March 1968 (in a game played at Maple Leaf Gardens) that saw Shack get a three-game suspension and a $300 fine and the Flyers defenceman a four-game suspension. Shack was well travelled in his career, which included stops with Los Angeles, Buffalo and Pittsburgh, but he did score 20 or more goals a year with five different teams. He finished his career in Toronto, where he was dealt back in 1973, and he totalled 239 goals and 465 points.

DAVE BALON

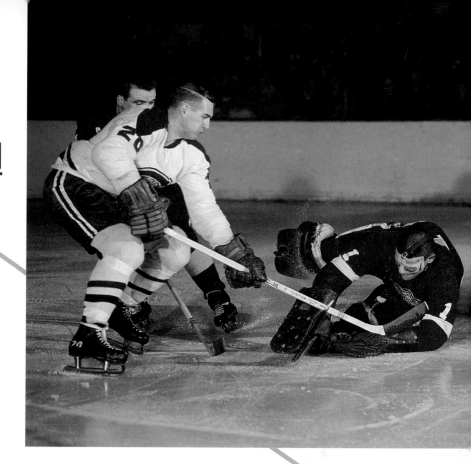

Montreal's Dave Balon (#20) moves in for a shot on Detroit goalie Terry Sawchuk (#1). Balon, a left winger, played just one full season with the New York Rangers in 1962-63 (11 goals, 24 points) before he was dealt to the Canadiens along with Leon Rochefort, Len Ronson and Gump Worsley in the trade involving Jacques Plante in June 1963. Balon responded with 24 goals for Montreal and followed up with 18 in 1964-65, when the Canadiens won the Stanley Cup. He contributed five points in nine games during the 1966 playoffs, when Montreal had a second consecutive triumph. After only 11 goals in 1966-67, Balon was drafted by the expansion Minnesota North Stars before returning to the Rangers in 1968-69. Never a great skater but a hard worker, Balon had a career high 70 points in 1969-70 and a best mark of 36 goals in 1970-71 while back in Manhattan. He played most of his last two NHL seasons in Vancouver in 1971-72 and 1972-73, recording a total of 22 goals for the Canucks.

The Money Game

A weekend road trip in 1961 (February 24-26) for Montreal Canadiens fans to New York City to watch their team play the Rangers cost $42.95 (tax included) by train, with tickets and hotel rooms. Those who attended saw the Habs defeat the Blueshirts 3-1.

FIRST GAME

Terry Sawchuk wore a mask for the first time to start the 1962-63 season. New York's Dave Balon was the only player to beat the Detroit goalie in a 2-1 Red Wings victory at Madison Square Garden on October 11, 1962.

TRIVIA

The Minnesota North Stars selected Dave Balon from Montreal as the first forward taken in the 1967 expansion draft. Oakland then took Bobby Baun (from Toronto), Pittsburgh took Earl Ingerfield (from New York), Los Angeles selected Gord Labossiere (from Montreal), St. Louis chose Jim Roberts (from Montreal) and Philadelphia picked up Ed Van Impe (from Chicago).

DON MARSHALL

New York's Don Marshall (#22) carries the puck while Rod Seiling (#16) watches. Marshall spent nine seasons with the Montreal Canadiens (1954-63) in the role of utility forward and superb penalty killer on the league powerhouse. He had 22 goals in 1957-58, and his best point total with the Canadiens was 46. Marshall was part of a major deal between Montreal and New York in June 1963 that saw Phil Goyette and Jacques Plante also join the Rangers. In New York, Marshall had four seasons of 20 or more goals and earned a second-team all-star berth in 1966-67 as a left winger. He scored 20 times for the expansion Buffalo Sabres in 1970-71 and played one last season for Toronto in 1971-72.

Rod Seiling was considered the top junior prospect in Canada when he played for the Memorial Cup-winning Toronto Marlboros. He played for the Canadian National Team at the 1964 Olympics (finishing fourth) and for Team Canada in 1972.

His NHL career stretched over 17 seasons with the Leafs, Rangers, Capitals, Blues and Atlanta Flames.

The Money Game

During the sixties, most NHL players had off-season jobs. The off-ice jobs of the 1964-65 New York Rangers included Vic Hadfield as a golf pro, Lou Angotti as an estimator and purchasing agent for a construction company, Bob Nevin as a hockey school instructor, Don Marshall and Phil Goyette as owners and partners of a bowling alley, Bill Hicke in public relations and Rod Seiling, Arnie Brown and Doug Robinson as university students.

For the 1963-64 season, the New York Rangers drew 497,978 fans to Madison Square Garden for 35 home games, although the team missed the playoffs. In 1992-93 the Rangers drew 738,968 fans to the new Madison Square Garden for 41 home dates, and the team once again failed to make the playoffs.

STATS

JACQUES LAPERRIERE

Montreal's Jacques Laperriere (#2) checks New York's Rod Gilbert (#7). The lanky Laperriere won the Calder Trophy in 1963-64, when the rookie defenceman scored two goals and had 28 assists to beat out teammate John Ferguson for the award. In 1965 he won the first of six Stanley Cups but missed the finals because he broke his ankle in the semifinals against Toronto. Laperriere bounced back in 1965-66 to win the Norris Trophy, scoring six times, racking up 31 points but missing the playoffs because of an injury. A four-time all-star, Laperriere recorded 242 assists in a 12-year career played entirely with Montreal. He returned to the Canadiens as an assistant coach and shared in two more Stanley Cups (1986, 1993).

TRIVIA

Jacques Laperriere is one of five Montreal Canadien defencemen to win the Norris Trophy. The other four are Doug Harvey, Tom Johnson, Larry Robinson and Chris Chelios.

The Money Game

The mid-sixties saw a number of how-to illustrated booklets produced. Available for 10 cents plus 10 liners from Coke or Sprite, the booklets featured players such as Jacques Laperriere on "How to play defence," Dave Keon on "How to play forward — defensive style," Henri Richard on "How to play forward -- offensive style" and Johnny Bower on "How to play goal."

TERRY HARPER

Montreal's Terry Harper (#19) is left bloodied after a fight with Toronto's Orland Kurtenbach during a March 1966 game at Maple Leaf Gardens. A willing but not always successful fighter, Harper began his NHL career in 1962-63 with the Canadiens when Tom Johnson was injured. The stay-at-home defenceman with a labouring skating style played his first NHL game against Detroit. The great Gordie Howe blocked a Harper shot and then broke in to score his 539th career goal. On October 30, 1963, Harper staged a wild brawl in Toronto with the Leafs Bob Pulford in the shared penalty box (recording 19 penalty minutes on his own), an event that led to the innovation of separate sin bins by November 8 at Maple Leaf Gardens. The 1963-64 season also saw Harper get 28 votes for the all-star team after he had two goals and 15 assists to go along with his 149 penalty minutes. He won five Stanley Cups in Montreal (the last in 1971) before going on to play for Los Angeles, Detroit, Colorado and St. Louis over 19 NHL seasons.

TRIVIA

The 1965-66 NHL Guide shows that Terry Harper (born in Regina) was one of many players who hailed from Saskatchewan. Other well-known NHLers from this prairie province who played in 1965-66 included Johnny Bower (Prince Albert), Bobby Baun (Lanigan), Bill Hay (Saskatoon), Glenn Hall (Humboldt), Ted Hampson (Togo), Gordie Howe (Floral), Dave Balon (Wakaw) and Red Berenson, Bill Hicke and Gary Peters (all from Regina).

MARKETING THE GAME

During the 1963-64 and 1964-65 seasons, Chex cereal featured posed colour photos – mostly of Toronto and Montreal players -- on the backs of their boxes. A few players from Detroit and Chicago were included as well. A total of 58 photos made up a complete set.

GORDIE HOWE

Detroit's Gordie Howe (#9) tries to tie up Toronto goaltender Johnny Bower (#1). During the sixties, Howe's role on the Red Wings was best described by Leafs player Dave Keon when he said, "There are four strong teams in the NHL and two weak ones. The weak ones are New York and Boston. The strong ones are Toronto, Montreal, Chicago and Gordie Howe!" The 1962-63 season saw Howe win his sixth (and final) Hart Trophy; he led the league with 38 goals and 86 points (for this great year, it was reported, Howe earned $29,000 in salary and $9,500 in league bonus money). By the end of the decade, Howe had become the all-time leader in goals scored (in 1963) and seasons played (in 1967); he had also recorded his 500th (in 1962), 600th (in 1965) and 700th (in 1969) career goals. Howe had the highest point total of his career at the age of 41, when he had 103 points in 1968-69 (44 goals, 59 assists). He played with the Red Wings until 1970-71, and he returned to the NHL for one season with the Hartford Whalers in 1979-80. Including his minor league totals, Howe scored 997 professional regular season goals in 2,238 games (a total that includes his one game appearance with Detroit of the IHL in 1997).

"Then there's the terrific NHL pension plan, the best in sports. When I'm 45 years old, I'll be able to collect $300 a month from the league for the rest of my life."

– *Gordie Howe* (Hockey News, *January 14, 1961*)

As part of the pension-surplus lawsuit settlement, Howe received $205,000 (in one lump sum). He had been getting approximately $13,000 a year as his NHL pension.

UNUSUAL NOTE

In 1965 the Detroit Red Wings played a game against the alumni team, with Gordie Howe and Ted Lindsay (who were both still active) playing for the old-timers. The game finished in a 6-6 tie, with Howe scoring three times for the alumni team before 12,037 fans. The alumni squad included Leo Reise, Harry Lumley, Marty Pavelich and George Gee.

STATS

Gordie Howe scored 801 goals in the NHL, and only two of them were scored on penalty shots. His second penalty shot goal was against his fishing partner, Johnny Bower, in a game on December 31, 1961, during a 4-2 Detroit win over Toronto. Howe scored 188 game-winning goals in his career.

RON ELLIS

Toronto's Ron Ellis (#8) gets knocked into the Detroit goal-mouth by Howie Young (#22). The Red Wings had shown an interest in Ellis, but he had always wanted to be a Maple Leaf and had even turned down a $10,000 scholarship from Michigan Tech, where he would have pursued an engineering degree. Instead, he joined the Toronto Marlboros and gunned 46 goals in 1963-64, when the team captured the Memorial Cup. The Marlies named Ellis as a co-winner of their MVP award (sharing it with Peter Stemkowski), and he was called up to the big club for one game in the 1963-64 season (against Montreal). The stocky winger made the Leafs in 1964-65, scoring 23 times and totalling 39 points. The first game of the year was played at the Detroit Olympia, and the 19-year-old Ellis had to go up against Ted Lindsay on his first shift. Ellis was the leading goal scorer when the Leafs won the Stanley Cup in 1966-67, with 22 tallies. A consistent goal scorer (11 straight seasons of 20 or more goals), Ellis had a career high of 35 in 1969-70. He spent his entire 16-season NHL career with Toronto, playing in 1,034 games and scoring 332 goals and 308 assists.

UNUSUAL NOTE

Howie Young was a noted brawler and tough guy and was known to cross-check opponents. He set an NHL record in 1962-63 with 273 penalty minutes in 64 games with the Red Wings. Young was also known for his legendary drinking habits (especially when with Detroit between 1961 and 1963), and he joined AA in June 1965 to save his career. The Red Wings took him back for the 1966-67 season, and he made this comment to *Hockey Pictorial* in February 1967: "This is the first time I ever woke up in Montreal without a hangover." He played in the NHL until 1970-71.

FIRST GOAL

Ron Ellis scored his first NHL goal against the Boston Bruins on October 17, 1964, at Maple Leaf Gardens. He beat goaltender Eddie Johnston, with the assists going to Bobby Baun and Andy Bathgate in a 7-2 toronto victory.

J. C. TREMBLAY

Montreal's J. C. Tremblay (#3) helps out goaltender Gump Worsley (#30) against Chicago attackers Doug Mohns (#11) and Ken Wharram (#17). Tremblay started out as a forward but moved back to defence when his skating would not allow him to keep up. He was first noticed as a professional with Hull-Ottawa of the EPHL in 1959-60, when he won the league's MVP award (which came with a $50 prize). He moved up to Montreal in 1960-61 to stay by showing what a good stickhandler he was and by playing smartly. In 1964-65 Tremblay had 20 points during the regular season and added another 10 in the playoffs to help the Canadiens take back the Stanley Cup. In the 1966 post-season, he had 11 points in 10 games as the Canadiens retained the Cup. Tremblay was quite upset that he lost out on the Conn Smythe to Red Wings goalie Roger Crozier. A flawless puck handler, he finally got all-star recognition in 1967-68 (second team) and in 1970-71 (first team). He finished with 363 points in 794 games for the Canadiens.

"I don't go for fights, brawls or perform like I'm in a circus when I'm on a hockey rink. My job is to help the team win. That's what I'm concerned with doing."

– J. C. Tremblay (Hockey News, *April 15, 1967*)

UNUSUAL NOTE

The Montreal Junior Canadiens played the 1964 Russian Olympic gold-medal-winning hockey team on December 11, 1964. Six members of the Quebec Aces (of the AHL) were added to the junior squad. Gump Worsley, Doug Harvey, John Hanna, Red Berenson, Leon Rochefort and Bill Sutherland were the six, but 15, 678 fans saw the Russians win 3-2. The contest was part of an eight-game tour by the Soviets (who went 7-0-1) and was played under international rules (defensive-zone bodychecking only). On December 16, 1965, the Junior Canadiens with Jaques Plante in goal beat the Russians 2-1.

The final NHL statistics for the 1967-68 season reveal that J. C. Tremblay recorded a league best of plus 28 in the plus-minus ratings.
Jean Béliveau was a plus 27, Jean Ratelle a plus 23, Yvan Cournoyer, Phil Esposito, Johnny Bucyk and Johnny MacKenzie all a plus 19, Phil Goyette a plus 18 and Dave Keon a plus 16.

BOBBY HULL

After coming close to breaking the 50-goal barrier in 1961-62, Bobby Hull (shown in the 1963 all-star game wearing #7) finally shattered the mark in 1965-66 when he blasted goal 51 past Cesare Maniago of the Rangers on March 12, 1966, at the Chicago Stadium. The assists on the goal went to Lou Angotti (the only helper Angotti had on Hull's 54 goals that season) and Bill Hay. Chico Maki had 16 assists on Hull's goals, whereas other prominent helpers included Stan Mikita (12), Phil Esposito (11), Pierre Pilote (11) and Pat Stapleton (9). Detroit goalie Roger Crozier allowed a high of nine Hull goals that year, followed by Montreal's Gump Worsley (7), Toronto's Terry Sawchuk (7), New York's Eddie Giacomin (6) and Boston's Eddie Johnston (5) and Cesare Maniago (5). A 10-time first-team all-star at left wing, Hull scored 604 goals for Chicago in 16 seasons before going to Winnipeg of the World Hockey Association (WHA) in June 1972.

"I mean as much to the Blackhawks as Willie Mays does to the San Francisco Giants. I believe I will ask for $100,000 next season."

– Bobby Hull speaking in 1965 (Hockey Illustrated, February 1968)

"He is a rare superstar who treats everyone alike: the coach, the players, the fans, the writers. He always has the time for everyone. He never cuts interviews short. He'll stand for an hour after a game signing autographs."

– Chicago coach Billy Reay on Bobby Hull
  (Hockey News, November 16, 1968)

The Money Game

One of the best hockey magazines produced during the sixties was *Hockey Illustrated* (which often featured colour action photos taken by Harold Barkley on the cover). A January 1967 issue with a Barkley cover photo of Bobby Hull and Bobby Baun sold for 50 cents. In addition to the many NHL player profiles, the magazine gave extensive coverage to the minor leagues. Back issues were available through an ad at the back of the magazine, and 10 could be bought for only $4. In 1964 Hull made a three-day appearance at the World's Fair signing copies of Hockey Illustrated with a photo of him on the cover.

UNUSUAL NOTE

Hockey did not get much exposure on American television during the sixties (except for the game of the week), but CBS did air a half-hour documentary entitled *This Is Bobby Hull* before a Chicago-Toronto playoff game on April 9, 1967.

PETER MAHOVLICH

Detroit's Peter Mahovlich (#11) tries to break through some Toronto checking. The Maple Leafs wanted to get Peter to play with his older brother Frank in Toronto, but the Red Wings drafted the younger Mahovlich second overall in 1963 (the first year an entry draft was held) from the St. Michael's Majors (who got $2,000 from the NHL club for developing the player). The Red Wings had high hopes for Mahovlich, who played in 34 games in 1966-67, scoring one goal and three assists. He scored his first NHL goal on November 6, 1966, in a 7-0 Detroit victory over Montreal, beating goalie Gump Worsley with a shot that trickled through the pads. Mahovlich needed more seasoning and was sent to Fort Worth of the Central Hockey League (CHL), where he put up good numbers (39 goals and 70 points in two years) before returning to Detroit in 1968-69. In June 1969, he was dealt to Montreal for Garry Monahan (who had been drafted first overall by the Canadiens in the 1963 draft). He had his greatest years in Montreal, winning four Stanley Cups (1971, 1973, 1976, 1977), and he was able to play with his brother between 1971 and 1974. He also played with Pittsburgh before returning to Detroit in 1979.

BROTHER ACT

Peter Mahovlich had five seasons of 30 or more goals (all with Montreal) in his career, whereas Frank had 10 seasons of 30 or more. The combined NHL goal total for the Mahovlich brothers is 821 (533 for Frank, 288 for Peter) and 1,972 points. The brothers were also together for Team Canada in 1972 and combined for 2 goals and 2 assists in the eight-game series.

STATS

In 1968 Peter Mahovlich was the tallest player in the NHL at six foot four inches. The smallest players were Yvan Cournoyer, Leo Boivin and Henri Richard, all only five foot seven inches. There were only 19 players over 190 pounds, and only nine were over 200 pounds (including Mahovlich at 210).

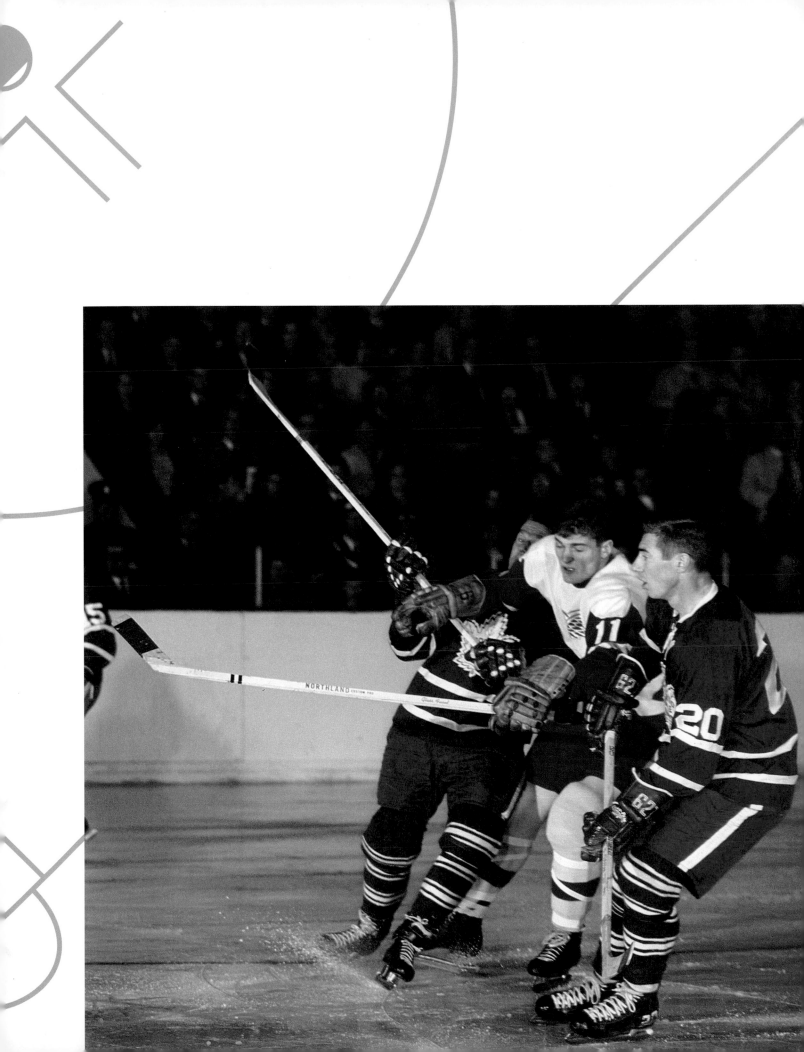

UNUSUAL NOTE

The New York Rangers played in Oakland on a Friday night (November 7, 1969) and were scheduled to play the Los Angeles Kings the following night at 8 p.m. at the Forum. However, the Forum had booked a Rolling Stones concert for the same time, and Kings management had neglected to tell the Rangers that they wanted to switch the hockey game to 2 p.m. Because they had not received enough notice, the Rangers initially refused, but they eventually relented when the Kings owner, Jack Kent Cooke, sent a private plane (at a cost of $4,000) to take the New Yorkers to Los Angeles right after their game in Oakland. The Rangers won the game 4-1, and Cooke got his $275,000 gate for the concert.

JEAN RATELLE

The future started to look good for the New York Rangers in 1960-61, when their top two junior prospects — Rod Gilbert and Jean Ratelle (#19) — finished first (with 103 points) and second (with 101 points) respectively in the OHA scoring race for the Guelph Royals. The same year, Ratelle had a three-game trial with the Rangers and scored his first NHL goal in his first game, beating Toronto goaltender Cesare Maniago. As promising as Ratelle was, he spent the next few seasons splitting his time between the minors and the Rangers while trying to overcome some serious injuries. By 1964-65 Ratelle was in New York to stay, and he had a breakthrough year in 1967-68, when he scored 32 times and assisted on 46 goals. He kept improving and scored a career high 46 goals in 1971-72 (winning the first of two Lady Byng Trophies) to go along with 109 points. Ratelle then had 41 markers in 1972-73 but was surprisingly traded to Boston (along with Brad Park and Joe Zanussi) in November 1975. The year of the trade saw Ratelle record 105 points. He played six seasons with the Bruins and finished a Hall of Fame career with 491 goals and 1,267 points.

STAN MIKITA

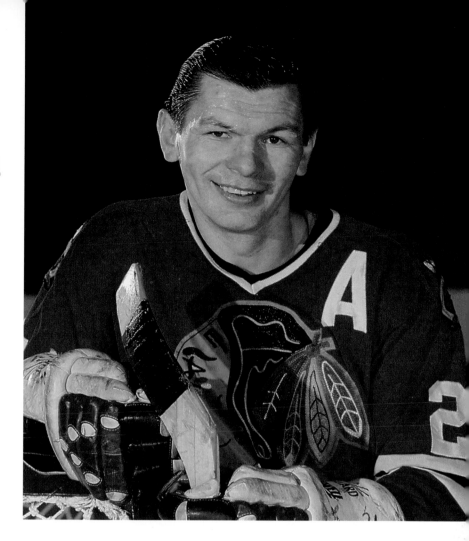

Chicago's Stan Mikita holds his famous curved stick for a photo. Mikita began experimenting with a curve in his (broken) stick while practising, and he quickly found that the puck could do funny things when struck with a "banana blade." Coupled with a change in attitude (a less belligerent Mikita decided to stay out of the penalty box), the Blackhawks centre began to accumulate impressive records and awards. In both 1966-67 and 1967-68, Mikita won hockey's "triple crown" in taking the Art Ross, Lady Byng and Hart Trophies by scoring a combined 75 goals, 109 assists and 184 points. He is only one of four players to win the Hart and Lady Byng in the same season (Buddy O'Connor, Bobby Hull and Wayne Gretzky are the others). A three-time first-team all-star, Mikita played his entire career in Chicago and holds the club record for most games (1,394), assists (926) and points (1,467) in 22 seasons.

"I think the toughest of them all may be Stan Mikita. He has so many moves and controls the play so completely when he is on the ice, it's next to impossible to cover him."
– Bobby Orr (Hockey News, *April 8, 1967*)

STATS

Many NHL players followed the lead of Stan Mikita and Bobby Hull and began using curved sticks. The results of using a curved stick were noticeable. Mikita's goals per season rose from 13.5 to 31 when he went to the new stick. Hull scored 101 goals in the four years prior to using a curved blade, but in the six years after the switch he scored 269 times or 44.8 goals per season. Rules restricting the amount of the curve (in 1967-68 and again in 1970-71) were implemented to protect goalies.

65

*"What's Imlach going to do with Sawchuk?
He has a great goalie in Johnny Bower."*

— *Gordie Howe* (Hockey News, *July 1964*)

*"He was fantastic. It's one of the best games I've ever seen
him play. Some of the saves were almost unbelievable."*

— *Punch Imlach on Terry Sawchuk after the fifth game of the semifinals
against Chicago* (Hockey News, *April 22, 1967*)

TRIVIA

The Maple Leafs used three goalies in one game on April 3, 1966,
during the final contest of the season. Johnny Bower, Terry Sawchuk
and Bruce Gamble all played in a 3-3 tie between Toronto and
Detroit at the Olympia. Bower left the game after the first period,
reportedly due to the flu.

TERRY SAWCHUK

In June 1964, the Maple Leafs surprised the hockey world by drafting goaltender Terry Sawchuk from the Red Wings (after having beaten him in the previous spring's Stanley Cup finals). Sawchuk proved to be a wise acquisition as he teamed with Johnny Bower to win the Vezina Trophy for the 1964-65 season. His final great moments came in the 1966-67 season. He recorded his 100th career shutout, on March 4, 1967, when the Leafs beat Chicago 3-0. Toronto got goals from Peter Stemkowski, George Armstrong and Bob Pulford, and Sawchuk made 22 stops. Sawchuk followed that up with an extraordinary performance in the playoffs, especially in game five of the semifinals versus Chicago. In a 4-2 Toronto win, he made a number of spectacular saves and consistently robbed Blackhawk snipers Bobby Hull and Stan Mikita. In the finals against Montreal, Sawchuk was again superb in winning the final two games of the series, including a remarkable effort in a 3-1 Cup-clinching win. It was Sawchuk's fourth Stanley Cup triumph (the previous three were with Detroit), and it made him only one of two goalies in NHL history to backstop two different teams to the championship (Patrick Roy is the other to do it with Montreal and Colorado). Sawchuk was the first goaltender taken in the 1967 expansion draft by the Los Angeles Kings.

Terry Sawchuk holds the NHL record of 103 shutouts. Seven of these shutouts were scoreless ties, five while he was with Detroit and two while he was with Boston.

ROGER CROZIER

"You're afraid, you're nervous, you don't know how well you're going to play. If I knew I'd play well every game, I wouldn't worry. I can't relax until the game's over."

– *Roger Crozier* (Hockey Illustrated, *January 1968*)

When nerves got the better of Crozier after two consecutive losses to Chicago during the 1964-65 season, the Red Wings sent him on a vacation to Miami Beach. He returned to beat Toronto 4-2 and had seven wins, two losses and two shutouts in his first nine games back.

The Money Game

The Red Wings finished in first place in 1964-65 and drew a team record 462,370 fans to the Olympia. Team management decided to upgrade the arena with a $1.5 million expansion, raising the number of seats by 2,312 to bring capacity to 16,375.

Detroit acquired goaltender Roger Crozier (#1) in a trade with Chicago in June 1963 that saw Howie Young go to the Blackhawks. Crozier played in 15 games for the Red Wings in 1963-64, recording two shutouts. In his first NHL game, on November 30, 1963, Crozier took a Frank Mahovlich shot in the face that broke his cheekbone, but he finished the game, which ended in a 1-1 draw between Detroit and Toronto. After the Red Wings lost Terry Sawchuk, Crozier became the primary goalie, and he responded with six shutouts (tops in the NHL) in 70 games in 1964-65. His performance earned him the Calder Trophy, even though Detroit was upset in the playoffs. In the 1966 playoffs, Crozier took the Red Wings to within two games of the Stanley Cup before losing to Montreal in overtime of game six of the finals. His acrobatics in the Detroit net earned him the Conn Smythe Trophy (the first time the award was given to a player on the losing team). Extremely nervous during his playing days, he retired briefly for health reasons in the 1967-68 season, but he did return to play for Detroit until 1969-70. His record with Detroit was 130 wins, 119 losses, 43 ties and 20 shutouts to go with a 2.94 goals-against average.

PAT STAPLETON

Pat Stapleton (#12) takes the puck away from the Chicago net, guarded by Denis DeJordy (#30). Stapleton and Leafs centre Dave Keon attended Detroit's junior tryout camp in 1956, and they were both sent home because they were too small. Stapleton did join the Chicago organization but was drafted by the Bruins in 1961 and played in 69 games for Boston in 1961-62. The next season, he only saw action in 21 games before going to the minors for the next three seasons. He was once again noticed by NHL teams when he was named the best defenceman in the Western Hockey League (WHL) with Portland. The Leafs acquired Stapleton in a trade on June 8, 1965, but lost him the next day to Chicago in the intraleague draft. Having found a home, Stapleton began to produce, increasing his assist total from 34 in 1965-66 to 50 in 1968-69 (an NHL record for defencemen at the time). He recorded six assists in one game on March 30, 1969, in a 9-5 Blackhawks win over Detroit (tying a mark for blueliners set by Babe Pratt in 1944). Stapleton was a three-time second-team all-star (1966, 1971, 1972) and was a member of Team Canada in 1972.

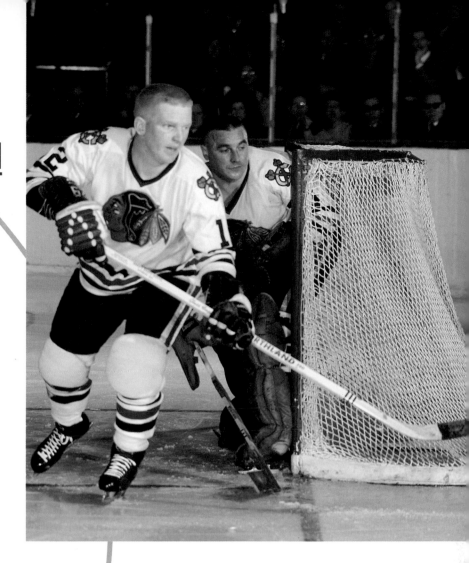

FIRST GOAL

Pat Stapleton scored a goal in his first game with the Chicago Blackhawks on November 28, 1965, at the Stadium. He scored the lone Chicago goal (assisted by Stan Mikita) in a 2-1 loss to Montreal by putting in a shot from the point. Stapleton's career marks as a Blackhawk show 286 assists and 327 points.

TRIVIA

Denis DeJordy's first NHL game was on November 7, 1962, the same night that Glenn Hall had to leave a game — with a back injury — for the first time after 502 consecutive starts in net. DeJordy took over at 10:21 of the first period, with the score tied 1-1, and the game finished 3-3. He had been sitting in the stands because the Blackhawks had called him up in case Hall's back gave out. He gained his first NHL victory in the next game, on November 10, 1962, in a 3-1 win over Montreal at the Forum. DeJordy shared a Vezina Trophy with Hall in 1966-67, and he played in Chicago until 1970.

69

EDDIE GIACOMIN

"Frank is a helluva guy. I hated to trade him. But I made the deal to help my hockey team."

– *Punch Imlach* (Hockey News, *March 16, 1968*)

FIRST SHUTOUT

Eddie Giacomin recorded his first NHL shutout on October 23, 1966, in a 1-0 win over Toronto. Ranger Wayne Hillman got the only goal of the game at 17:14 of the third period.

Marketing the Game

Available in 1969 were full-colour posters of favourite NHL stars, such as Bobby Orr, Bobby Hull, Gordie Howe, Gump Worsley, Red Berenson and Eddie Giacomin, at a cost of $2 each.

New York goalie Eddie Giacomin (#1) has Toronto winger Frank Mahovlich (#27) to contend with at the side of the net. Giacomin kicked around in the minor leagues for a number of years and finally gained some recognition with Providence of the American Hockey League (AHL). Detroit and Toronto both tried to pursue Giacomin, but it was the Rangers who gave up five players to the Providence team and gained the goaltender's services. He started out by playing in 35 games for New York in 1965-66 (splitting the duties with Cesare Maniago). By 1966-67 he was the starting goalie for the Rangers and had a league high of nine shutouts to gain a berth on the first all-star team. Giacomin again led the NHL in shutouts (eight) for the 1967-68 season, and he returned to the first all-star squad in 1970-71. He played with the Rangers until 1975, when the Red Wings picked him up on waivers in a move that was highly unpopular with New York fans. The Hall of Famer still holds the Rangers club record for most career shutouts with 49, and his sweater number was retired.

Frank Mahovlich had 260 career goals by 1966-67 (an average of 29 a year) and was a six-time all-star (twice on the first team), but he was still traded by the Leafs in 1968 to the Red Wings. Toronto was offered $1 million for Mahovlich by Chicago owner Jim Norris in 1962, but the club turned the offer down (although Harold Ballard and Stafford Smythe seriously considered it for a couple of days). Leafs coach Punch Imlach once squabbled with Mahovlich over $500 on a contract, and the "Big M" held out for a while. His salary in 1963-64 was estimated to be $25,000.

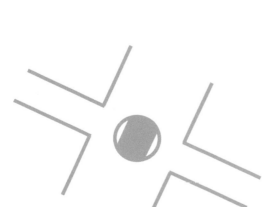

JOHN FERGUSON

Montreal's John Ferguson (#22) crashes into Toronto goaltender Johnny Bower (#1) with defenceman Larry Hillman (#22) looking to jump clear of the pileup. Ferguson made his NHL debut in dramatic style on October 8, 1963, by getting into a fight just 12 seconds into the game (against Ted Green) and then scoring two goals in a 4-4 tie at Boston. The hard-nosed left winger was doing exactly what the Canadiens wanted him to do. Montreal management was tired of seeing the club's smaller players getting pushed around and liked the fact that Ferguson was an intense competitor (while with Cleveland of the AHL, he once fired a puck at a teammate during a warm-up because the other player was not being serious in preparing for the game). Ferguson was much more than a brawler, scoring 18 times as a rookie while totalling 45 points and racking up 125 penalty minutes. His best year in the NHL was in 1968-69, when he scored 29 goals and then posted a league record of 80 penalty minutes in the 1969 playoffs. Ferguson won three resounding playoff fights (in 1965 against Eric Nesterenko, in 1966 against Eddie Shack, in 1968 against Ted Green) in years that the Canadiens won the Cup. In 500 career games, Ferguson recorded 303 points and 1,214 penalty minutes.

"Johnny is the most remarkable athlete in professional sport. Show me another man half his age [44] who fills a job as tough as playing goal in the NHL. I don't think you can find one."

– *Punch Imlach on Johnny Bower*
(Hockey Illustrated, *February 1968*)

TRIVIA

In 1995 the Maple Leafs honoured goaltending legends Turk Broda and Johnny Bower by raising their sweater number (#1) to the rafters at Maple Leaf Gardens. Other "honoured" Leaf numbers include Syl Apps, Charlie Conacher and George Armstrong (all with #10), Ted Kennedy (#9) and King Clancy and Tim Horton (both with #7). The numbers for Bill Barilko (#5) and Ace Bailey (#6) have been permanently retired.

GERRY CHEEVERS

Gerry Cheevers (#30) was a top goalie in the Toronto system from 1959 to 1965, winning championships with St. Michael's (OHA) and with Rochester (AHL). He played his first two NHL games as a Maple Leaf in 1961-62, going 1-1-0 (giving up seven goals) and then never played for Toronto again. Although the Leafs tried desperately to keep Cheevers on their protected list (even claiming that he was a forward because he had played on the wing for three weeks when he was with St. Michael's), the Bruins drafted him in June 1965 for $30,000. He didn't become a Boston regular until 1967-68, but it was worth the wait as Cheevers took the Bruins to a couple of Stanley Cups (1969 and 1972). He played in 416 regular season games for Boston, winning 229 to go with a 2.89 goals-against average and 26 shutouts. Note that his mask is dotted with stitch marks, which he said he would have received if it weren't for the facial protection.

"Toronto had Johnny Bower who was playing well for them and then in 1964 they picked up Terry Sawchuk in the draft. I knew there was no way I was going to win a job from a pair of greats like that. They left me unprotected and Boston grabbed me for the draft price. I was glad of it."

– *Gerry Cheevers* (Hockey Pictorial, *April-May 1969*)

The Money Game

During the 1965 intraleague draft, the Bruins spent $120,000 to improve their team by drafting Gerry Cheevers (from Toronto), Paul Popeil (from Chicago) and Norm Schmitz and Keith Wright (both from New York). Only Cheevers proved to be worth the investment.

FIRST SHUTOUT

Gerry Cheevers recorded his first NHL shutout against his former team by making 31 saves in a 4-0 Bruins win over the Maple Leafs on November 10, 1966, at the Boston Garden. He was helped by Murray Oliver, Johnny Bucyk, Pit Martin and Wayne Connelly, who scored the goals.

MIKE WALTON

Mike "Shakey" Walton was part of the great Toronto Marlboros hockey club that won the Memorial Cup in 1964, and he earned 46 points in the playoffs. He then won the award for rookie of the year in the Central League with Tulsa and then in the American League with Rochester. Walton made it to the NHL in 1966-67, splitting that year between Toronto and Rochester but sticking around for the playoff run, which saw him record 7 points in 12 games as the Leafs won the Stanley Cup. The 1967-68 season was his first full year in the NHL, and he scored 30 times and added 29 assists. He was named one of the three stars of the game for seven straight home contests between November 15 and December 9, 1967. Walton received $100 for his 10th and 15th goals that year and then $100 for every goal after 20. The Leafs gave him $23,000 for the 1968-69 season. He stayed in Toronto until 1971, when he was dealt to Boston (where he won a second Stanley Cup in 1972). Walton then jumped to the WHA, where he was a top scorer for many years, before returning to the NHL with Vancouver, Chicago and St. Louis. His NHL totals show 588 games played with 201 goals and 448 points.

TRIVIA

Mike Walton was a member of the Calder Cup-winning Rochester Americans (AHL) in 1965-66. The Maple Leafs farm club might have been as good as a couple of NHL teams and was loaded with former and future big leaguers such as Gary Smith, Larry Jeffrey, Jim Pappin, Bobby Perreault, Gerry Ehman, Al Arbour, Ed Litzenberger, Duane Rupp, Bronco Horvath and Brian Conacher. Also on the team was future Boston coach and *Hockey Night in Canada* commentator Don Cherry. In 1967 the Leafs sold their AHL franchise for $400,000 and their WHL Victoria franchise for $500,000, beginning the decline of their hockey dynasty.

The Money Game

During the mid-sixties, the Ontario legislature voted (by a 40-8 count) against allowing the Maple Leafs to increase the capacity of Maple Leaf Gardens by 4,000 seats because the club would have had to build two overhangs over adjoining streets and thereby set a dangerous precedent. In June 1997, the Leafs couldn't get local politicians at Toronto's city hall to agree that their Union Station proposal for a new arena was worth the $34 million they wanted to pay and not the $100 million requested by the city. In February 1998, the Leafs announced that they would finally be getting a new downtown home, to be called the Air Canada Centre.

KEN HODGE

Boston's Ken Hodge (#8) is checked by Toronto's Tim Horton (#7). A big, strong right winger, Hodge used his size (six foot one, 200 pounds) to good advantage and could unleash a hard, accurate shot. He scored 63 goals for St. Catharines of the OHA, making him a top prospect of the Chicago Blackhawks. In his first two full years in Chicago, Hodge managed to score 16 goals but was then traded to Boston along with Phil Esposito and Fred Stanfield. After a 25-goal year in 1967-68, Hodge scored 45 goals and made 45 assists in his second season with the Bruins. A one-time 50-goal scorer (in 1973-74), he set a team record for right wingers in a season with 62 assists and 105 points in 1970-71. He scored 289 career goals as a Bruin but was dealt to the New York Rangers in 1975.

Despite a Hall of Fame career, Tim Horton never won the Norris Trophy (finishing second two times), and he was not named to the first all-star team until 1967-68 (repeating in 1968-69). His 24-year NHL career included stops in New York, Pittsburgh and Buffalo.

"Twenty goals is the first cutoff point in judging whether a man has had a good year. I feel that I can make it this year."
– *Ken Hodge* (Hockey Pictorial, *April-May 1968*)

"Horton's the hardest bodychecker I've ever come up against. He's as strong as an ox and hits with terrific force."
John Ferguson (Hockey News, *May 13, 1967*)

UNUSUAL NOTE

On January 3, 1965, Ken Hodge (19 years old) scored two goals in a 4-3 loss for St. Catharines in an afternoon junior game at Niagara Falls, Ontario. He then travelled to Buffalo and played that evening for the Bisons (Chicago's farm club) of the AHL in a game against the Cleveland Barons. Hodge assisted on the last goal of the game (scored by Ed Van Impe) in a 9-4 Buffalo win. It was Hodge's first professional hockey game.

GILLES TREMBLAY

Montreal's Gilles Tremblay (#21) tries to put one past Toronto goaltender Terry Sawchuk. Tremblay broke into the NHL as a rookie in 1960-61 with the Canadiens. He scored his first goal on November 13, 1960, in a 2-1 Montreal win at Madison Square Garden by beating Rangers netminder Gump Worsley with a shot to the far corner of the net after taking passes from Bernie Geoffrion and Jean Béliveau. Tremblay generally played defensive hockey first, but the Canadiens told the left winger that he had to score if he wanted to stay in the NHL. He listened and scored 32 goals in 1961-62 (the fifth best total in the league that year) and added 25 and 22 markers in the next two years. A broken leg cut short the 1964-65 season, but Tremblay came back to score 27 goals in 1965-66 and then chipped in nine points in 10 playoff games in the Canadiens run to the Stanley Cup. He scored 23 goals in 1967-68 and totalled 51 points for his contribution to another Cup win. His last season was 1968-69, which ended for him after 44 games and 10 goals due to an injury. He finished with 330 points in 509 games.

The Money Game

Gilles Tremblay of the Canadiens and Reg Fleming of the Blackhawks engaged in a stick-swinging duel on October 24, 1962, at the Chicago Stadium. The combatants took eight to 10 swings at each other, though neither player was seriously injured. Both were suspended by league president Clarence Campbell for three games involving Montreal and Chicago, and they were fined $750 apiece, to which Campbell added an extra $100 each.

WALTER TKACZUK

Ranger Walter Tkaczuk (#18) battles Leaf Ron Ellis for position. In his final year of junior hockey in Kitchener, Tkaczuk recorded 93 points in 52 games, and New York was counting on the German-born centre to help the club out of the NHL's lower echelon. He spent only a few games in the minors before playing in 71 games for the Rangers in 1968-69, scoring 12 goals. In only his second season, Tkaczuk finished fifth in league scoring, with 27 goals and 50 assists. He played his entire 14-year career in New York, totalling 227 goals and 678 points in 945 games.

STATS

The New York Rangers captured the final play-off spot for the 1970 postseason on the strength of a 9-5 win over Detroit in the last game of the 1969-70 schedule. The Rangers fired 65 shots at Red Wings goalie Roger Crozier in a desperate attempt to overtake the Montreal Canadiens on goal differential. The Canadiens only scored twice in their final game against Chicago. The Rangers made the playoffs because they scored 246 goals, two more than the Canadiens.

TED HARRIS

A native of Winnipeg, Ted Harris (#10) of the Canadiens first got recognition in the AHL in 1963-64, when, playing for the Cleveland Barons, he won the Eddie Shore Award as the best defenceman. He spent six years in the minors (mostly in Springfield) and developed a tough reputation by frequently recording over 100 penalty minutes in a season. The Canadiens acquired his rights in a trade and brought Harris up to stay in 1964-65. He scored his first NHL goal on December 5, 1964 (his only goal of the year), by taking a pass from Claude Provost and drilling it past Chicago's Glenn Hall in a 5-3 Montreal win. He added 14 assists and 107 penalty minutes as a rookie. In the 1965 playoffs, Harris tied a record set by his one-time mentor Eddie Shore by recording four penalties in one period of a playoff game against Toronto. A second-team all-star in 1967-68, Harris won four Stanley Cups in Montreal before going to Minnesota and Philadelphia (where he won another Cup in 1975).

"He taught me how to play the man and the puck. I figure he made me more versatile."

– Harris on his minor league coach, Eddie Shore
(Hockey Pictorial, *December 1966*)

The Money Game

Eagle Toys of Montreal first began selling table hockey games in 1954. The company signed the Montreal Canadiens to an agreement to use their uniform and logo. A deal with the Maple Leafs – and eventually deals with the other four NHL clubs – followed. Each team was to receive an estimated $7,500 for its permission. The game came in seven different models that sold from $5 to $20. By 1964 the company was selling 175,000 games per year all over the world.

STATS
The 1968-69 Montreal Canadiens broke the 18-year-old Detroit Red Wings record of 101 points by finishing the season with 103 (46 wins and 11 ties in 76 games). The 1976-77 Canadiens set the current NHL record of 132 regular season points (60 wins and 12 ties in 80 games).

BOBBY ORR

Boston's Bobby Orr (#4) checks Toronto's Rick Ley (#2) from getting too far into the Bruins zone. It has been estimated that Orr received $55,000 for a two-year contract and another $25,000 as a signing bonus with the Bruins in September 1966. (In 1997 the Bruins gave the first pick of the entry draft, Joe Thornton, a $925,000 salary per year and a signing bonus of $462,500.) The dollars Orr received were unheard of at the time, but he was no ordinary 18-year-old prospect. In his final year of junior hockey in Oshawa, Ontario, Orr had 38 goals and 56 assists for 94 points while playing defence, but he was edged out for the OHA's MVP award by André Lacroix. Orr's numbers left the cellar-dwelling Bruins drooling at the thought of this phenomenon joining their team. Tough negotiations ensued between the Bruins and Orr's agent, Alan Eagleson, making the defenceman the first significant player to use a lawyer to hammer out a contract. Orr never disappointed the Bruins, winning the Calder Trophy in 1967 (13 goals, 28 assists), three Hart Trophies (1970, 1971, 1972), two Art Ross Trophies (1970, 1975) and two Conn Smythe Trophies (1970, 1972) in the years Boston won the Stanley Cup. Although his career was relatively short due to injuries, Orr did it all and is arguably the greatest player ever to play the game. One thing is certain: Orr changed the way defencemen play the game, making blueliners part of the attack. He was also the first Canadian-born athlete to be named *Sports Illustrated*'s Man of the Year (in 1970).

"Hey Emms, why don't you trade Orr? He's making the rest of the Bruins look bad."

– *Boston fan to Bruins general manager Hap Emms* (Hockey News, *March 4, 1967*)

TRIVIA

Bobby Orr won the first of eight straight Norris Trophies in 1967-68 by gaining 68 points in the voting to second-place finisher J. C. Tremblay's 31. Others to get points included Tim Horton (30), Jim Neilson (26), Jacques Laperriere (15), Pierre Pilote (11), Bill White (9), Mike McMahon (8), Ted Green (6), Harry Howell (5), Gary Bergman (4), Pat Stapleton (1), Ed Van Impe (1) and Kent Douglas (1).

STATS

Bobby Orr still holds the NHL record for most points in a season for a defenceman, with 139 in 1970-71. Paul Coffey is next, with 138 in 1985-86 for Edmonton. Orr (135 and 122) and Coffey (126) also hold the next three highest totals for blueliners. Orr was the first defenceman to score three goals in one playoff game, on April 11, 1971, against Montreal. This record has been tied nine times since.

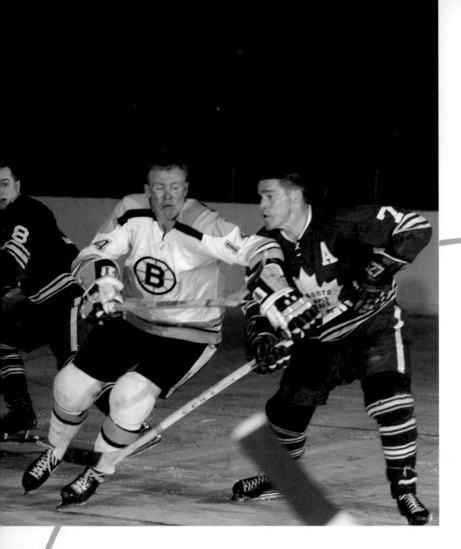

GLEN SATHER

Boston's Glen Sather (#14) tries to get away from the checking of Toronto's Tim Horton. A hard-nosed checker and penalty killer, Sather was Detroit property, but the Bruins drafted the left winger in June 1965. He made his NHL debut in 1966-67, when he played in five games for the Bruins. His first full year was 1967-68, which saw him score eight goals and add 12 assists in 65 games. Sather missed out on the Boston Stanley Cup win of 1970 because he was drafted by Pittsburgh and then sent to the New York Rangers. Sather also played in St. Louis, Montreal and Minnesota, totalling 658 career games, with 80 goals and 113 assists. Since retiring as a player, Sather has entrenched himself in Edmonton, where he coached or managed the Oilers to five Stanley Cups. As a coach, he won 464 regular season games (.616 winning percentage) and 89 playoff games (.706 winning percentage).

"He's a handy guy to have around. If anyone gets hurt he can play either wing and he is always hustling. He's a good man on the ice killing penalties. It's true you can't call him a goal scorer but he is strong on defence."

– *Boston coach Harry Sinden on Glen Sather*
(Hockey News, *March 2, 1968*)

DENNIS HULL

Chicago's Dennis Hull (#10) charges in front of the Toronto goal. Hull was a prized prospect when he scored 48 goals for St. Catharines of the OHA in 1963-64. He played with the Blackhawks in 1964-65, scoring 10 goals in 55 games as a rookie. He scored his first NHL goal at the Montreal Forum on December 19, 1964, by taking a pass from Eric Nesterenko and firing a 10-foot shot past Charlie Hodge in a 6-3 victory. He split the next season between St. Louis (in the CHL) and Chicago but returned to stay in the NHL in 1966-67, when he had 25 goals. Known for his high, hard shot, Hull was the first player to shatter the glass at the Chicago Stadium, during a game against Montreal. In 1968-69 he had his goal total up to 30 and his point production up to 64. Hull had his best seasons in the seventies playing with Jim Pappin and Pit Martin. He made the second all-star team in 1972-73 and scored a total of 298 career goals for the Blackhawks to go with 640 points. Hull played one season in Detroit (1977-78) before retiring.

TRIVIA

The 1963-64 OHA junior "A" league first all-star team featured future NHL players Bobby Orr and Doug Jarrett on defence, André Boudrias at centre, Yvan Cournoyer on right wing and Dennis Hull at left wing.

Unusual Note

A 1967 survey showed that 68 percent of NHL players had lost at least one tooth to hockey. Seventy percent of NHL defencemen were denture wearers, 63 percent of goalies and 57 percent of forwards. Sticks caused 56 percent of the damage, and pucks were blamed for tooth loss 30 percent of the time. Mouth guards, first developed by Pierre Lemontague at the University of Montreal, helped to reduce these numbers significantly over the years.

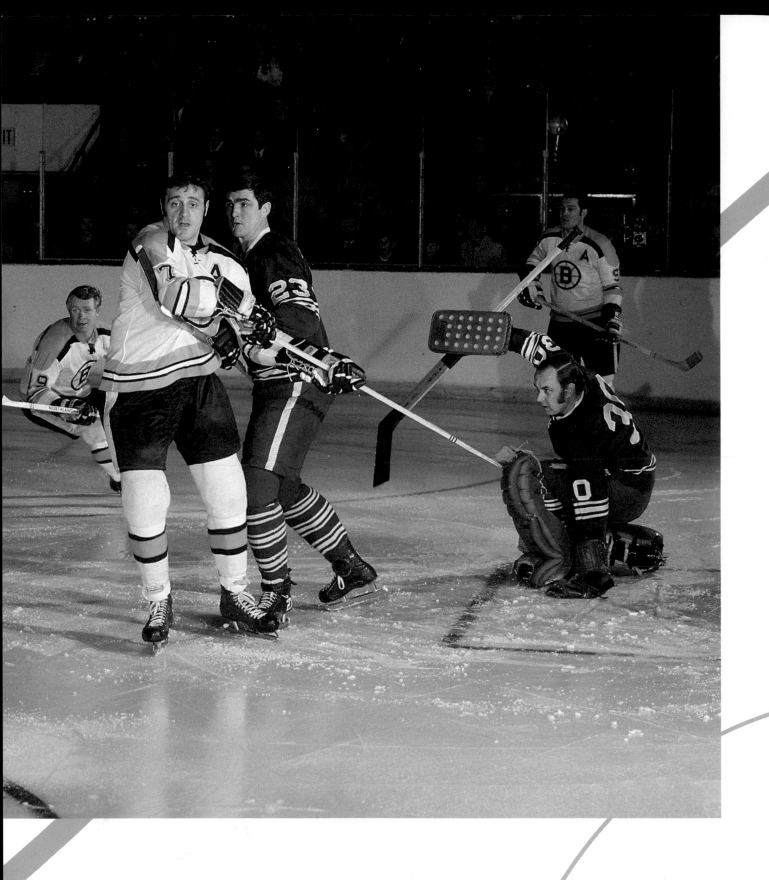

PHIL ESPOSITO

Boston's Phil Esposito (#7) battles in front of the net with Toronto's Pat Quinn (#23). Esposito's first attempt at winning a scoring championship came in junior "B" when he played in Sarnia, Ontario, and had 47 goals and 61 assists. However, he finished second in the scoring race by two points to Terry Crisp. After a three-year stay in Chicago in which he scored 74 goals for the Blackhawks, Esposito became a big-time point producer and goal scorer for the Boston Bruins after a May 1967 trade. He finished second to Stan Mikita in the 1967-68 scoring race, but he won the first of five Art Ross Trophies in 1968-69, when he became the first player to record 100 or more points in a season (126). In 1970-71 Esposito also set a new record by scoring 76 goals, a record that lasted until Wayne Gretzky scored 92 in 1981-82. Dealt to the Rangers in 1975, Esposito finished with 717 career goals and 1,590 points. Both Esposito (New York Rangers and Tampa Bay) and Quinn (Vancouver) became NHL general managers.

"I'm not aggressive enough and my skating isn't very good. I have the weight but I don't throw many body checks and I should shoot the puck more often."

— *Phil Esposito* (Hockey Pictorial, *March 1966*)

"I realized I'd get more ice time with the Bruins and if I scored well for them in the long run, I could make more money than with Chicago."

Phil Esposito (Hockey News, *October 28, 1968*)

TRIVIA

The Central Professional Hockey League (CPHL) began operations in 1963-64 and instituted a rule that each team must have 10 players not older than 23. Future NHL players who played in the CPHL's first season included Phil Esposito (St. Louis), Claude Larose (Omaha), Gary Dornhoefer (Minneapolis), Ernie Wakely (Omaha), and Bob Plager (St. Paul). By 1965-66 the top ticket price for the St. Louis Braves was $3.

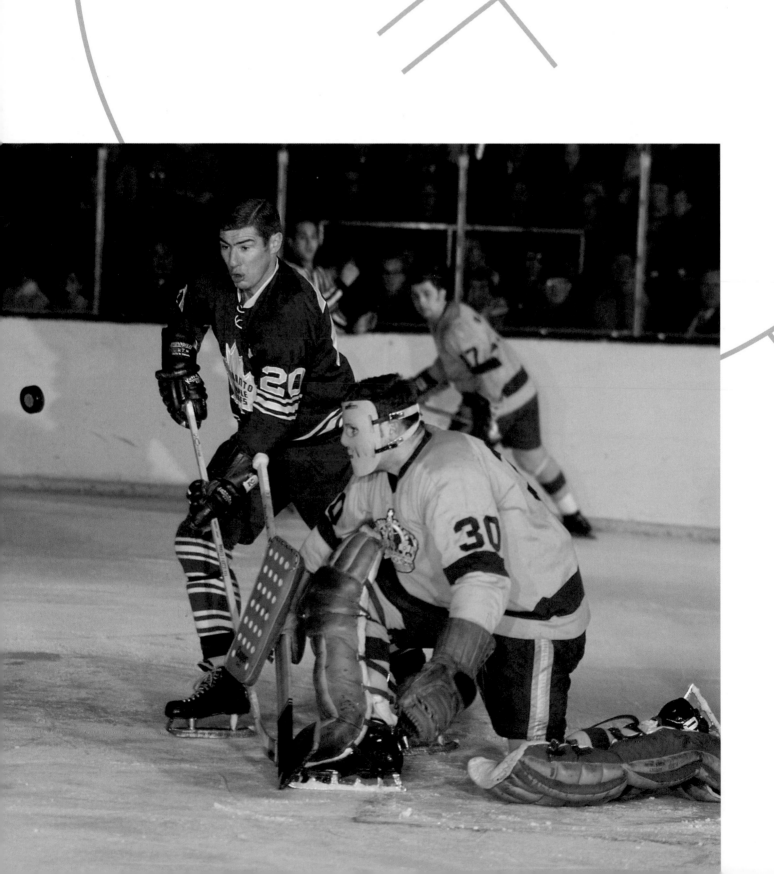

BOB PULFORD

Toronto's Bob Pulford (#20) waits for a shot at Los Angeles Kings goaltender Gerry Desjardins (#30). Pulford was one of the NHL's top checkers and clutch performers in 14 seasons with the Maple Leafs. His best year was in 1965-66, when he scored a career high 28 goals and 56 points. His playoff totals with Toronto were 25 goals and 26 assists in 89 games. He was named captain of the Kings after a 1970 trade to Los Angeles. Pulford was also named the first president of the NHL Player's Association in 1967, and he believed that such a union would benefit both the players and the game.

A native of Sudbury, Ontario, Gerry Desjardins was the property of the Montreal Canadiens before being dealt to the Kings for two first draft choices in 1969 and 1972 (which they used to select Hall of Famer Steve Shutt). Known as "the fastest glove in the West," Desjardins played in 60 games in his first year in Los Angeles (1968-69), recording four shutouts and a 3.26 goals-against average while replacing the legendary Terry Sawchuk. Desjardins recorded his first NHL shutout on November 6, 1968, in a 2-0 Los Angeles victory at home against the New York Rangers.

"This is not the east or mid-west. When did you ever see a boy with a hockey stick in Southern California? We really are introducing the sport here. And we are right on schedule. It will be a great success."

– *Jack Kent Cooke, the first owner of the Los Angeles Kings* (Hockey News, *March 2, 1968*)

TRIVIA

In the 1964 playoffs, Bob Pulford had five goals and eight points as the Maple Leafs won their third consecutive Stanley Cup. His performance won him — in an informal poll of sportswriters and two coaches — MVP of the playoffs (edging out Gordie Howe of the finalist Red Wings). The unofficial vote took place because NHL president Clarence Campbell wanted reaction to the idea of naming a playoff MVP. A year later, the Conn Smythe Trophy, honouring the long-time Maple Leafs owner and manager, was adopted to recognize the best player of the postseason. Others considered to name the award after were Lester Patrick (who did have a trophy named in his honour in 1966 for those who give "outstanding service to hockey in the United States") and one-time Leafs hero Bill Barilko.

"The Rocket was everything in hockey to me. I guess it was the same for most kids in Montreal. He was the greatest who ever lived. How could I compare to him?"

— Yvan Cournoyer on his childhood hero Maurice "Rocket" Richard, a player he was often compared to early in his career
(Hockey Illustrated, *January 1968*)

FIRST GOAL

Yvan Cournoyer scored his first NHL goal during a five-game trial with the Montreal Canadiens in 1963-64. The goal came against Detroit's Roger Crozier on October 27, 1963, at the Olympia, with Cournoyer putting in his own rebound in a 6-4 Montreal win. In his five-game trial, Cournoyer scored four goals.

The Money Game

In 1966 the six NHL teams were faced with the following equipment costs: $365.35 to outfit a goalie (a mask was $25, and a pair of pads went for $84), $3.25 for a stick ($5 for a goalie stick), $25 for shin pads and $60 for skates.

YVAN COURNOYER

In his final season of junior hockey, Yvan Cournoyer (#12) scored 63 times to lead the Ontario Hockey Association (OHA) in goals during the 1963-64 season, making him a sure bet for NHL stardom. He did not disappoint, spending only seven games in the minors (with Quebec of the AHL) before returning to stay with the Canadiens for the 1964-65 season. He began his NHL career as a power play specialist, scoring 16 of 18 goals in 1965-66 with the extra man. The first 11 of these goals came on just 28 shots on goal. Cournoyer turned in seasons of 25 and 28 goals before leaping to 43 in 1968-69. He was reportedly earning $18,000 a year in 1968 and drove a $7,000 Stingray convertible. "The Roadrunner" led the Canadiens in goals scored five times in his career (with a high of 47 in 1971-72), and he was a four-time second-team all-star left winger. A clutch playoff performer, Cournoyer shared in 10 Stanley Cups with the Canadiens (winning the Conn Smythe Trophy in 1973) and finished with 428 career goals and 863 points in 968 games. He was inducted into the Hall of Fame in 1982.

DEREK SANDERSON

Boston Bruin Derek Sanderson (#16) searches for a loose puck against Leafs goalie Bruce Gamble (#30). Sanderson became a hot prospect when he won the OHA scoring title with 101 points in 1966-67 for Niagara Falls. He beat out future NHLers such as Mickey Redmond, Jim Lorentz, Garry Monahan and Garry Unger for first place. The colourful, long-haired centre played an agitating style that made him a marked man in opposing arenas. But Sanderson could play good hockey as well, winning the Calder Trophy in 1967-68 (24 goals and 25 assists as a rookie) and becoming one of the top penalty killers in the league. (In 1969 he became the first player to score three short-handed goals in a playoff year.) It was Sanderson who put a perfect pass on Bobby Orr's stick for the famous Stanley Cup-winning goal of 1970. In 391 career games for Boston, Sanderson recorded 294 points. He also played for New York, St. Louis and Vancouver before retiring and later becoming a Bruins broadcaster.

Bruce Gamble began his NHL career with the Rangers and played with the Bruins before joining Toronto in 1965-66. In eight games that season, Gamble recorded an amazing four shutouts.

"I don't think the officials watch me as much here as they did in Niagara Falls. I got a reputation for being rough and I was. I was in a lot of fights and I did pull quite a few tricks. But I knew I couldn't get away with things up here so I've concentrated more on just playing the game. My goal always has been to get here. Now that I am here, I want to stay here."

– *Derek Sanderson* (Hockey News, *December 2, 1967*)

The Money Game

The Boston Bruins gave Derek Sanderson a three-year deal to start his career that called for payments of $10,000, $12,000 and $13,000. Bruce Gamble was once fined $50 in 1961 for missing a practice (it was the second largest fine ever handed out by Bruins coach Milt Schmidt to that point), and he was once given $200 by Leafs coach and general manager Punch Imlach for shaving his sideburns.

GORDON "RED" BERENSON

"It was a freak, a fluke. It was great for hockey but I just keep telling myself something like that isn't in character for me. A few good plays or stopping the opposition from scoring, that's my game. But six goals . . . it's ridiculous."

– *Red Berenson* (Hockey Illustrated, *January 1970*)

The Money Game

Red Berenson turned down a $16,000 offer from the Montreal Canadiens to complete his education at the University of Michigan. He may have made up for it somewhat when St. Louis held a special night for him on November 17, 1968 (in honour of his six-goal game). Among other gifts, he received a station wagon, a hunting rifle and a canoe. (Berenson was an avid outdoorsman.)

The Western Division came into existence with the six-team expansion of the NHL for the 1967-68 season. All the new teams were placed in this division, whereas the "original six" formed the Eastern Division. A champion from each would play for the Stanley Cup. In 1967-68 the Western Division had a record of 40-86-18 against the established clubs. The Western Division teams played more games against the Eastern Division teams in 1968-69 and finished with a record of 51-129-36. The St. Louis Blues represented the Western Division in the finals for three straight seasons but couldn't win a single game. The playoff format was changed, and Chicago moved to the Western Division in 1970-71.

S T A T S

Gordon "Red" Berenson (#7) began his NHL career with the Montreal Canadiens in 1961-62 and was with the Habs when they won Stanley Cups in 1965 and 1966. He was dealt to New York in 1966-67 and played 30 games that year for the Rangers without getting a goal (and only five assists). A trade to the St. Louis Blues the following year gave Berenson a new life, and he scored 22 goals and had 51 points in 55 games. In 1968-69 he tallied 35 goals and had 82 points to lead all Western Division scorers (and eighth overall). On November 7, 1968, he scored six goals against Philadelphia's Doug Favell in an 8-0 Blues victory over the Flyers. In 1969-70 Berenson proved that the previous year was no fluke by scoring 33 goals and 72 points. In 987 games, Red Berenson scored 261 goals, the first of which came in 1961-62 with the Montreal Canadiens. On March 25, 1962 (the last night of the season), Berenson scored on a power play by picking up a Bernie Geoffrion pass behind the net and then coming out in front and backhanding a shot into the Detroit net. The Canadiens won the game 5-2. He was also one of the first players to wear a helmet.

"I had to quit . . . I'm 56 years old. The pressure was getting to be unbearable. The day of the game, I was getting to be unbearable. The afternoons were the worst. All the thinking. And then the waiting, waiting, waiting."

— *Toe Blake* (Hockey News, *December 14, 1968*)

UNUSUAL NOTE

Referee Eddie Powers quit his job when NHL president Clarence Campbell fined Toe Blake only $200 for saying after a February 1963 game, "The officials handled the game as though they had a bet on it." Powers resigned on February 15, 1963, because he felt that the league was not supporting him with such a light fine for remarks detrimental to hockey. (Campbell once fined Blake $2,000 for punching referee Dalton McArthur after a 1961 playoff game in Chicago.) In the 1997 playoffs, Canadiens defenceman Dave Manson was fined $10,000 when he commented on the officiating, in particular the work of referee Stephen Walkom, in a game during the Montreal–New Jersey series. Manson was not suspended, but the Canadiens lost the series.

HECTOR "TOE" BLAKE

Montreal coach Hector "Toe" Blake ended his legendary career behind the Canadiens bench in 1968 after four Stanley Cup wins in the sixties (1960, 1965, 1966, 1968). His career, which spanned 914 games between 1955 and 1968, saw him win 500 times, lose 255 contests and tie another 159 for a winning percentage of .634. He never missed the postseason in his 13-year coaching career, winning 18 of 23 series and 82 of 119 playoff games. His NHL record for coaches of eight Cup wins has been equalled by Scotty Bowman, but Blake remains the only coach to have won all eight with the same franchise.

ED VAN IMPE

Flyers defenceman Ed Van Impe (#2) and goalie Doug Favell (#1) combine to stop Maple Leaf Paul Henderson (#19). The rugged Van Impe finished second to Bobby Orr in the 1966-67 Calder Trophy race when he was with the Chicago Blackhawks. Van Impe was also one of four original Flyers selected in the expansion draft of 1967 to be a member of the Stanley Cup teams of 1974 and 1975 (the others were Bernie Parent, Gary Dornhoefer and Joe Watson).

In their first season, the Flyers finished atop the Western Division with 73 points, then a record. The current record for the highest season points total by an expansion club in its first season belongs to the 1993-94 Florida Panthers (83 points).

"Good thing I'm already married. I'd never get a girl now with this face."

– Ed Van Impe on fracturing his cheek and taking 16 stitches after stopping an Alex Delvecchio blast (Hockey News, *December 28, 1967*)

FIRST GOAL

Paul Henderson scored "The Goal" with 34 seconds to play in Moscow to win the 1972 Summit Series. His first NHL goal came as a Detroit Red Wing versus Chicago goaltender Glenn Hall in a 2-2 tie on January 29, 1964. Taking passes from Parker MacDonald and Pit Martin, Henderson drove a shot over Hall's shoulder to tie the game. The goal came one day after Henderson turned 21. In 13 NHL seasons with Detroit, Toronto and Atlanta, Henderson scored 236 goals and 477 points in 707 games.

AL ARBOUR

Al Arbour (#3) was named the first captain of the St. Louis Blues to start the 1967-68 season. An experienced winner (Stanley Cups with Chicago and Toronto), Arbour was excellent defensively but still split his time between the minors and the NHL from 1952 to 1967. He was named the AHL's most outstanding defenceman for 1964-65, when he was with Rochester (in the Toronto system), with one goal and 16 assists. Arbour stood out by wearing glasses, which he decided to put on after chasing a broken stick blade (in a junior game), thinking it was the puck. The play was up the ice, and Arbour was by himself at the other end. Despite wearing glasses, he became a superb shot blocker, learning his lessons from Red Wings and Maple Leafs great Bob Goldham. Arbour went on to have a great coaching career with the New York Islanders, winning four Stanley Cups between 1980 and 1983. He ranks second to Scotty Bowman in coaching victories, with 781.

"We've done well against the old teams because we have experienced leaders who played with the old ("original six") teams for years and weren't awed by them. It is better for young players to break in surrounded by older players. Older players are generally the best players in the NHL anyway. We're approaching parity within a few years I think."

– *St. Louis Blues coach Scotty Bowman* (Hockey Pictorial, *November 1969*)

The Money Game

In their first year of operation, the St. Louis Blues paid $2 million for the franchise, $3.75 million for the arena they played in, $2.25 million to refurbish the rink and $225,000 in payroll. The Blues finished with a 27-31-16 record in 1967-68 and made the Stanley Cup finals. On May 7, 1968, the Blues played the second game of the finals at home and drew 16,179 fans (a 1-0 loss to Montreal). The World Series-champion St. Louis Cardinals played the New York Mets the same night at home and drew just over 9,000 fans.

SERGE SAVARD

Serge Savard (#18) spent 1966-67 with Houston of the Central League and won rookie of the year award, with seven goals, 25 assists and 155 penalty minutes. He edged out future NHLers such as Al Hamilton, Wayne Cashman and teammate Rogie Vachon for the award. He also played in two games for the Montreal Canadiens that year (no points) and joined the big club for good the next season, playing in 67 contests. He scored his first NHL goal against Bruins netminder Gerry Cheevers, who was so upset that he tossed the puck into the crowd. An usher returned the puck to Savard. In the 1969 playoffs, the young defenceman won the Conn Smythe Trophy, with 10 points in 14 playoff games as the Canadiens swept the St. Louis Blues to win the Stanley Cup. Despite his outstanding play year after year, Savard only made the all-star squad once in his career (second team in 1978-79). An excellent playmaker, he recorded 312 assists in his career as a Canadien. He is a member of the Hall of Fame.

UNUSUAL NOTE

The Montreal Canadiens talked about a new arena for 1967 to go along with the Expo '67 project so as not to duplicate effort and waste money. "The project is at the study stage only, and so far the study has centred only on the economic and civic benefits which such a venture would bring to the World's Fair, the city of Montreal and the Canadien Arena Company," said Canadiens owner Senator Hartland Molson (*Hockey News*, February 1, 1964). The Canadiens did not get their new arena (the Molson Centre) until March 1996.

FIRST GOAL

Serge Savard won seven Stanley Cups in his playing career, scoring 19 goals and 49 assists in 130 playoff games. His first playoff goal came on May 7, 1968, against the St. Louis Blues in a 1-0 Canadiens victory. Claude Provost set up the marker, which won the second game of the finals, in which the Canadiens swept the Blues. Montreal has won the Stanley Cup 23 times, and on six of those occasions the club has swept the finals in four straight games.

LES BINKLEY

Pittsburgh goalie Les Binkley (#30) has to contend with Toronto's Peter Stemkowski (#12). Binkley started out as a trainer with the Cleveland Barons of the AHL in 1960-61 and only practised as a goaltender. When he replaced starter Gil Mayer and won six games in a row, he saw a career in the net develop. He was named rookie of the year in the AHL in 1961-62 but stayed in the minors until 1967-68. Binkley believed that his wearing contact lenses would scare away NHL clubs, but the Pittsburgh Penguins gave the 32 year old a chance in their first season, and he came through with six shutouts (topped only in 1997-98 by Tom Barrasso with seven) in 54 games to go with a 2.88 goals-against average. He was the first goalie from an expansion team to beat an established club when the Penguins beat Chicago 4-2 on October 21, 1967. He played in Pittsburgh until 1971-72 before going to the WHA for four more seasons.

Peter Stemkowski's greatest moments came in the 1967 play-offs for the Stanley Cup-winning Maple Leafs when he had 12 points in 12 games as a centre between Bob Pulford and Jim Pappin.

Marketing the Game

Pittsburgh's NHL franchise had some 350 names submitted in 1966-67 to help name the team. Favourites included Hornets (the name of their AHL team), Penns, Panthers and Quakers. Penguins was ultimately selected.

UNUSUAL NOTE

Peter Stemkowski played 15 NHL seasons with Toronto, Detroit, New York Rangers and Los Angeles, scoring 206 goals in 967 games. He readied himself for retirement by being a disc jockey in his native Winnipeg while he played for the Leafs. Aspiring to be a broadcaster, he said: "I realize I'll have to study to prepare myself and that's what I'm going to do" (*Hockey News*, March 4, 1967). Stemkowski was the television colour commentator for the San Jose Sharks between 1992 and 1996.

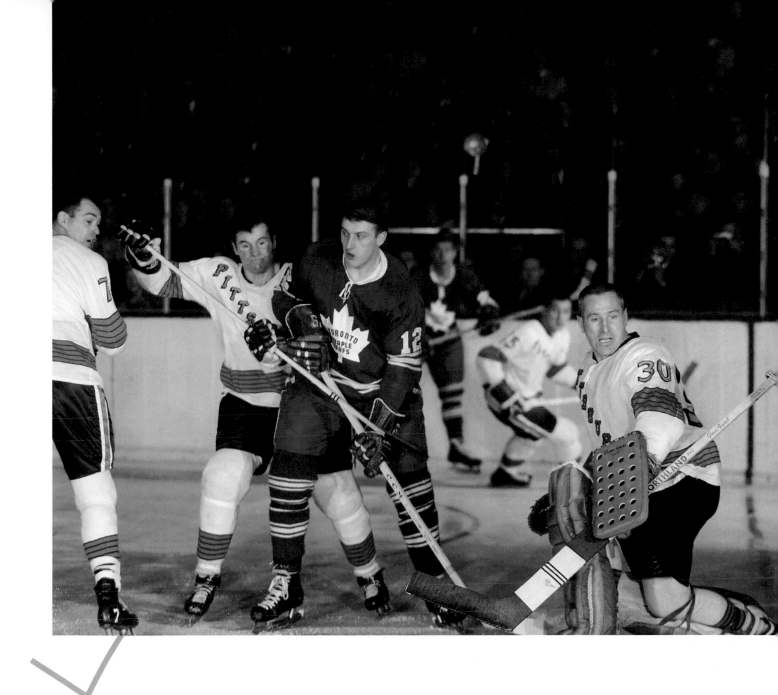

BILL WHITE

The Money Game

On October 1, 1966, the Chicago Blackhawks played an exhibition game in Los Angeles against the minor league Blades of the WHL. Chicago won the game 6-2 in front of Hollywood stars such as Edgar Bergen (in attendance with his daughter Candice), Andy Williams, Debbie Reynolds, David Janssen, Janet Leigh, Glenn Ford, Dean Martin, Steve Allen, Ryan O'Neal, Groucho Marx, Doug McClure and Adam West. Most came to see Blackhawks star Bobby Hull, who did not disappoint and scored a goal.

UNUSUAL NOTE

During their first year in the NHL, the Los Angeles Kings had a nine-year-old mascot named Kevin Sloan, who skated with the team in pregame warmups wearing sweater number 13. The Kings also had ladies night (half-price tickets for women) and hockey stick night (1,000 sticks available to all kids under the age of 16).

Los Angeles Kings defenceman Bill White (#21) languished in the minors for many years before expansion gave him a chance at the NHL. Once the property of Toronto, he was dealt to Springfield of the AHL as part of a five-player package the Leafs gave up for Kent Douglas in 1962. White stayed in Springfield until 1967, when the Kings purchased the farm team and brought him up to the big league club, just in the nick of time for White. "Life in Springfield under Eddie Shore wasn't very pleasant and if it hadn't been for the opportunity to move to the NHL with Los Angeles this season, I think I'd have retired," White said (*Hockey News*. December 16, 1967). He scored 11 goals and 27 assists in 1967-68, making good use of his size (six foot two, 190 pounds), strength and puck-handling. White had 33 points the next season but was dealt to Chicago in 1970, where he made two trips to the finals with the Blackhawks (1971, 1973). He was an important defender on Team Canada in 1972.

JACQUES LEMAIRE

In typical Montreal Canadiens style, centre Jacques Lemaire (#25) spent his first year as a pro developing his skills with the Houston team in the CPHL even though he was a top junior prospect (93 points in 48 games in his last junior season, 1965-66). He went to Houston and scored 19 goals and 49 points while he worked on his defensive game. Lemaire became a Canadien in 1967-68 and started out with 14 goals in his first 37 games (finishing with 22), stepping up to take a major role when Henri Richard was injured. Playing on a line with Bobby Rousseau and Dick Duff, the hard-shooting Lemaire finished second to Derek Sanderson in the Calder Trophy race. In the 1968 playoffs, Lemaire scored two overtime winning goals and had 13 points in 13 games as the Canadiens won the Stanley Cup. A clutch playoff performer, Lemaire scored 61 postseason goals and added 78 assists, which helped him to win eight Stanley Cups as a player. He played his entire NHL career in Montreal between 1967 and 1979, scoring 366 goals and 469 assists in 853 games. Lemaire came back to coach the Canadiens in 1983, and he won another Cup as coach of the New Jersey Devils in 1995.

"He can play in the league as long as he wants."

– Chicago coach Billy Reay on Jacques Lemaire
  (Hockey News, May 4, 1968)

Marketing the Game

The 1968-69 season was the final year that Shirriff Foods issued hockey coins (Jacques Lemaire is coin number F-14 in a complete set of 176). Each coin had a full-colour head-and-shoulder shot of a player or coach on the front. The first issue of the coins came in 1960-61, and the second issue came out in 1961-62 and was available in Salada Tea and Shirriff Dessert packages and potato chip bags. The 1962-63 issue was the first to feature metal coins.

STATS

Jacques Lemaire never scored fewer than 20 goals a year in his entire NHL career (12 years — his highest total was 44 in 1972-73), a record that he shares with Bill Barber (12 seasons and Mike Bossy (10 seasons). Both these players — except for Lemaire — were named as NHL all-stars, but the Canadiens centre is in the Hall of Fame, as are Barber and Bossy.

GARY SMITH

Toronto's Murray Oliver (#11) celebrates a goal put past Gary Smith (#30) of the Oakland Seals, while defenceman Carol Vadnais is unable to help. Smith began his NHL career with the Maple Leafs (playing five games for them), and he startled a national television audience when he skated with the puck to the Montreal Canadiens blueline in a December 21, 1966, contest. The Leafs lost 6-2, but Smith's rush sent a buzz through the NHL (the league later implemented a rule to prohibit goalies from crossing the centre redline). The Seals claimed Smith in the 1967 expansion draft, and he played in 21 games in 1967-68 for the Oakland club. He played in 54 contests the next season, recording four shutouts and a 2.97 goals-against average. His workload increased to 65 and then to 71 games by 1970-71, his last season as a Seal. A trade sent him to Chicago, where he played behind Tony Esposito until 1972-73. Smith also played for Vancouver (he still holds the Canucks team record for most shutouts in a season, with six), Washington, Minnesota and Winnipeg. Always ready to travel, Smith was nicknamed "Suitcase."

TRIVIA

Carol Vadnais played in 11 games for the Montreal Canadiens in 1966-67 and did not retire until 1982-83 after playing in 1,087 games for Oakland, Boston, New York Rangers and New Jersey in addition to his games for the Habs. He was the second-to-last player to retire from the "original six" era. The last was Boston's Wayne Cashman, who played in one game for the Bruins in 1964-65. Cashman left the NHL after the 1982-83 season, playing his entire 1,027-game career with Boston.

UNUSUAL NOTE

In addition to their regular training camp goalies (including Gary Smith), the Toronto Maple Leafs had the Czechoslovakian national team goaltender Vladimir Dzurilla attend their preseason workouts in September 1965. He was the same goaltender whom future Maple Leafs great Darryl Sittler would beat to win the first Canada Cup tournament, held in 1976.

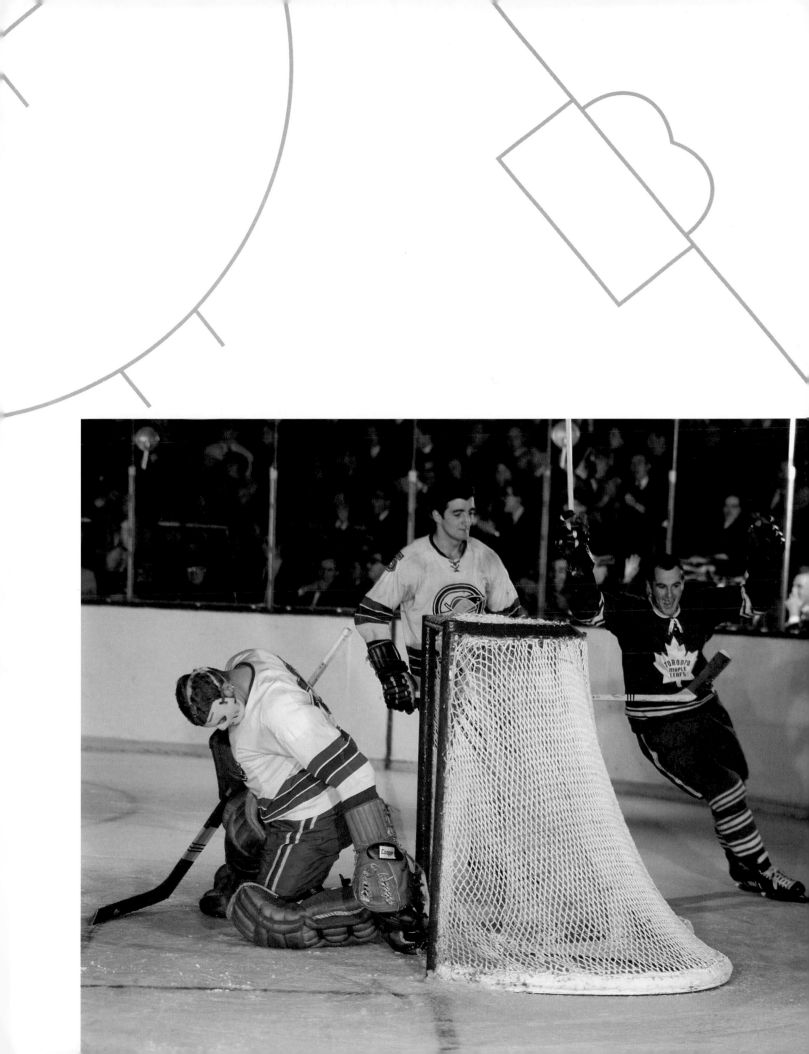

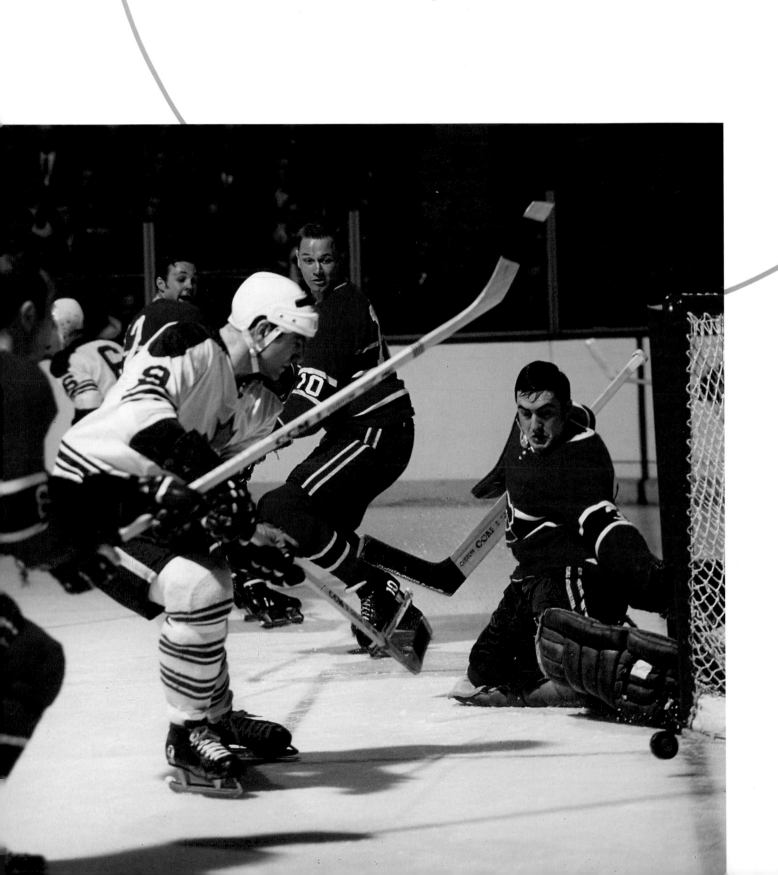

ROGATIEN VACHON

Montreal goaltender Rogatien Vachon (#29) stops Toronto's Norm Ullman (#9). Vachon's NHL career started in 1966-67, when Canadiens regular goalie Gump Worsley was injured. In his first game, he faced Gordie Howe and the Red Wings on February 18, 1967, at the Forum. Just three minutes into the game, Vachon was forced to stop Howe on a breakaway, and, benefitting from goals by Claude Provost, Claude Larose and Dave Balon, he won the game 3-2. Toronto coach Punch Imlach was still not impressed with Vachon and said prior to the 1967 finals, "Canadiens beat us? They'll never beat us with a junior 'B' goaltender." Imlach's reference was to Vachon's playing junior hockey with the Thetford Mines Canadiens in 1964-65. Although Vachon played well in the finals, the Leafs did win the Cup. However, Vachon was not discouraged, coming back to share the Vezina Trophy with Worsley in 1967-68 and then taking the Canadiens to their second consecutive Cup win in 1969, allowing only 12 goals in eight playoff games. He was dealt to Los Angeles and made the second all-star team twice (1975, 1977) with the Kings. Vachon also played for Detroit and Boston, but his greatest moment came in the 1976 Canada Cup when he was named the best goalie of the tournament.

FIRST SHUTOUT

Rogie Vachon recorded a total of 51 career shutouts, the first 13 of which came with the Montreal Canadiens. He recorded his first shutout on March 5, 1967, at Madison Square Garden in New York. The young netminder turned back 29 Ranger shots in a 2-0 Canadiens victory, on goals by Yvan Cournoyer and Bobby Rousseau.

MARKETING THE GAME

Let's Talk Hockey was an instructional record album put out by the Toronto Maple Leafs and RCA-Victor in 1966. It featured tips from Andy Bathgate, Dave Keon, Johnny Bower, Tim Horton and coach Punch Imlach. Aimed at kids between the ages of seven and 17, the album was 44 minutes long and was available for $4.10 (including postage) or could be purchased from Maple Leaf Gardens.

The Money Game

In 1966-67 the Montreal Forum installed 408 new lights so that games could be broadcast in colour on television. The cost was over $300,000, and the floor underneath the ice surface had to be repainted to help reduce glare. The Forum was completely remodelled in 1968 at a cost of $10 million and reopened its doors on November 2, 1968, when the Canadiens edged the Red Wings 2-1.

CLAUDE LAROSE

"Players have to give everything they've got every minute of every game. Some just aren't psychologically able to do it. They want to but it's just not in them. They're being paid and paid well to do it. If they don't, they have to be punished."

— John Muckler, coach of the North Stars
(Hockey News, *January 11, 1969*)

The Money Game

The North Stars picked green as a primary uniform colour because the home state of Minnesota was known for its trees, forests and grass. They thought about a blue-and-white combination, but it belonged to the Maple Leafs.

TRIVIA

During the sixties, the minor leagues had many coaches who eventually moved up to the NHL then or in the seventies. This group includes Fred Shero, Bobby Kromm, Joe Crozier, Johnny McClellan, John Muckler, Harry Sinden, Fred Glover, Johnny Wilson, Keith Allen, Don Perry, Claude Ruel, Fred Creighton, Larry Popein and Al MacNeil. Five of these coaches won a Stanley Cup (Ruel, Sinden, MacNeil, Shero, Muckler).

Minnesota's Claude Larose (#15) takes a shot on Leafs goalie Bruce Gamble. Larose was dealt to the North Stars by the Montreal Canadiens (along with Danny Grant) in June 1968. Larose had his best season in 1968-69, with 25 goals and 37 assists while playing on a line with Grant and Danny O'Shea. "I wouldn't trade that line for the whole St. Louis team" said Minnesota coach John Muckler (*Hockey Illustrated*, November 1969). Despite having 24 goals and 47 points in 1969-70, Larose was traded back to Montreal (for Bobby Rousseau) to start the 1970-71 season. The deal gave Larose an opportunity to win a third Stanley Cup as a member of the Canadiens. He finished his NHL career with St. Louis, totalling 483 points in 943 games. His son Guy has played in the NHL with Winnipeg, Toronto, Calgary and Boston since the 1988-89 season.

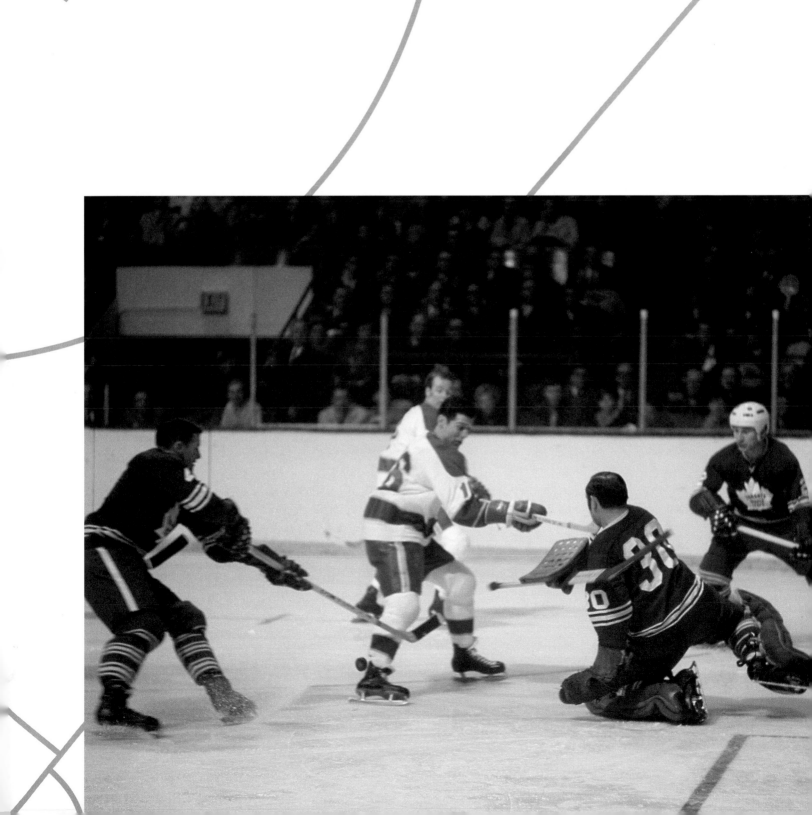

GEORGE ARMSTRONG

Seals captain Ted Hampson (#10) battles George Armstrong of the Leafs for control of the puck.

George Armstrong was a plodding skater but still effective in patrolling the right wing for the Maple Leafs, especially during the playoffs. In the club's Cup-winning years, Armstrong supplied 37 points in 45 playoff games and scored his most memorable goal (the last of the "original six" era) into an empty Montreal net to close the last game of the 1967 final. Armstrong played his entire career in Toronto and was captain of the Leafs for a record 12 straight years (1957-58 to 1968-69). Only Steve Yzerman of Detroit has served as many in a row (1986-87 to 1997-98 and counting). The next longest consecutive-serving captains include Alex Delvecchio (11 seasons between 1962-63 and 1972-73 with the Red Wings), Bill Cook (11 seasons between 1926-27 and 1936-37 for the Rangers), Hap Day (10 seasons between 1927-28 and 1936-37 for the Maple Leafs), Jean Béliveau (10 seasons between 1961-62 and 1970-71 for the Canadiens), Rod Langway (10 seasons between 1982-83 and 1991-92 for the Washington Capitals) and Ray Bourque (10 seasons and counting since 1988-89 with the Bruins).

"Us old guys are playing for our jobs. If we lose, Punch will have to rebuild and that means guys like me will have to go. I don't kid myself."

– *George Armstrong* (Hockey News, *April 17, 1965*)

Hampson began his NHL career in 1959-60 with Toronto after the Leafs claimed his rights from the New York Rangers. The Blueshirts reclaimed Hampson in June 1960, and he played three years on Broadway. Detroit drafted him in 1963, and he had a good year in 1966-67, with 13 goals and 48 points for the Red Wings. The next season saw him dealt to the Oakland club, and he totalled 54 points (27 for the Red Wings, 27 for the Seals). Before the 1968-69 season, Hampson was named captain of the Seals (who finished second that year in the Western Division), and he responded to the challenge by scoring 26 goals and 49 assists (the second-best point total in his division). He was named the winner of the Masterton Trophy, edging out Jim Roberts of St. Louis for the award. For being the Seals MVP, the *Oakland Tribune* newspaper awarded him a $500 prize. A small but pesky checker throughout his career, Hampson was dealt to Minnesota in 1971, where he finished his playing days.

George Armstrong is one of six players to have captained a team to the Stanley Cup four or more times. The leader is Jean Béliveau with five, and Armstrong is tied with Maurice Richard, Yvan Cournoyer, Denis Potvin and Wayne Gretzky at four each. Mark Messier is the only player to have captained two different teams to the Stanley Cup (Edmonton Oilers and New York Rangers).

TONY ESPOSITO

Dave Keon of Toronto (#14) back-hands a shot past Montreal goal-tender Tony Esposito (#1) for a goal on December 11, 1968, in a 4-4 tie at Maple Leaf Gardens. Esposito went to college at Michigan Tech instead of playing junior hockey, and he began his professional career with Vancouver of the WHL in 1967-68. He split 1968-69 between Houston and Montreal, where he played in 13 NHL games. Esposito got into his first game when Rogie Vachon was injured on November 29, 1968 (in a 5-4 loss at Oakland), when he played the last 26 minutes of the match. He rebounded to win his first game on December 7, 1968, by defeating Chicago 6-3 at the Forum.

Not a favourite of Canadiens coach Claude Ruel, Esposito was drafted by the Blackhawks in June 1969 (at a cost of $30,000), and he began a stellar career in the Windy City. He was named rookie of the year in 1969-70, recording a modern NHL record of 15 shutouts in the regular season to go with a 2.17 goals-against average. Esposito's unorthodox butterfly style and great catching hand earned him three Vezina Trophies and three first-team all-star selections. He was elected to the Hall of Fame in 1988.

"Tony is a fighter, not a shot gets by him that he doesn't get sore at himself. One minute he's shooting the puck down the ice in disgust and the next minute he's making a great save."

– *John Ferguson on teammate Tony Esposito*
(Hockey News, *December 28, 1968*)

FIRST SHUTOUT

Tony Esposito recorded 76 career shutouts (seventh highest all-time total), and his first came at the Montreal Forum on December 14, 1968, in a 1-0 win over Philadelphia. He stopped 35 shots and outduelled Flyers goalie Bernie Parent, who blocked 46 of 47 shots on goal.

TRIVIA

When Tony Esposito won both the Calder and the Vezina Trophies in 1970, he became only one of two goaltenders to win both awards in the same season. Frank Brimsek of the Boston Bruins (1939) was the other. Pittsburgh's Tom Barasso (1984) and Chicago's Ed Belfour (1991) also won both awards in the same year, but the Vezina had been changed in 1982 to a trophy given to the goalie "who is judged to be the best at his position" rather than to the netminder(s) who allowed the fewest goals.

AFTERWORD

In 1961-62 Bobby Hull hit the magic 50-goal mark, but not until the 70th and final game of the season. Yet, try as he might, he couldn't overcome that barrier with another goal in the game. The next season saw him get an ordinary (for him) 31 goals, but in 1963-64 he notched 43 tallies in a 70-game schedule. It seemed certain that Hull would pass the 50-goal mark, but the 1964-65 season produced for him "only" 39 goals in 61 games (he lost nine games due to an injury). Now, in 1965-66, Hull (who began the year with two goals in the first game of the season, a 4-0 Chicago win at Maple Leaf Gardens) was poised for another assault on the record he shared with Maurice Richard and Bernie Geoffrion. By the 57th game of the season, Hull had reached the 50-goal plateau for the second time in his career. Amazingly, the next three games saw him and the Blackhawks shut out completely with 5-0, 1-0 and 1-0 losses to Toronto, Montreal and New York respectively. There were nine games to go, and fans wondered if Hull would be denied again.

March 12, 1966, saw the New York Rangers visit the Chicago Stadium. There would be no better time for Hull to get goal 51 than in front of the hometown fans. But Rangers goalie Cesare Maniago was having no trouble turning away shots from the Chicago left-winger. At 4:05 of the third period, New York's Harry Howell picked up a penalty for slashing, with the Blackhawks trailing 2-1. A power play opportunity might just do the trick for Hull. Bill Hay and Lou Angotti managed to get the puck to Hull, who, with his fluid and forceful stride, skated across the Rangers blueline and forced the defensive pairing of Jim Neilson and Wayne Hillman to retreat. Once in the attacking zone, Hull took a quick look around. He noticed teammate Eric Nesterenko, a strapping right-winger, heading for the front of the net in the hope of distracting or screening Maniago. Conditions were just right for Hull to unleash his lethal slapshot. He wound up and put his entire body into the blast, and with a blur it was past the netminder. Goal 51 was Hull's at long last!

Pandemonium broke out as the puck hit the back of the Rangers net. Then fans stopped breathing for a moment, wondering if Nesterenko had tipped the shot, but it had been Hull's all the way from just inside the blueline. The sell-out crowd of about

"There's physical pressure but it's the mental strain of an entire year that kills you when you're going for a record."

— *Bobby Hull*
(Hockey Illustrated, *November, 1966*)

**S
T
A
T
S**

Bobby Hull's great shot helped him to lead the NHL in goals scored a total of seven times, including five seasons of 50 or more goals. His highest total was 58 in 1968-69 when he also had a career best of 107 points.

22,000 went wild, showering the ice with just about everything they could get their hands on. Hats, programs and other debris rained down as the ovation lasted some eight minutes. Hull skated over to shake the hands of all his teammates, who were standing at the bench. He then went over to kiss his wife, who was seated in the front row behind the glass in the Chicago end. Hull put his hand to his lips and then touched the glass. His wife kissed the glass in return while photographers captured the moment. As Hull skated back to the bench, he picked up one of the hats that littered the ice and put it on his head at a jovial angle while the crowd roared its approval. Anyone at the game probably doesn't even remember that Chicago won the contest 4-2.

To understand how significant Hull's achievement was at the time, consider that only two players scored 50 or more goals in the entire decade of the sixties (Hull, Geoffrion), whereas the seventies saw 50 or more goals scored 31 times and the eighties saw the mark reached or bettered 76 times. Hull's achievement was thus the single greatest hockey highlight of the sixties, leaving an indelible mark on an epoch of superior hockey. The sixties were the highlight of hockey's "Golden Era" (the years between 1942-43 and 1966-67), and with good reason. The calibre of hockey had never been higher, with all the players able to master the fundamentals of skating, shooting and passing. The players had been well trained in the respective "systems" of the six teams. The goaltending was handled in stellar fashion by six men (though more were added when the two-goalie system was implemented). Every shutout was well earned, as was every goal. Each player had to come prepared to play, because an eager and talented minor leaguer was hungry to take an NHL job. The fierce competition meant no nights off and few dull games. The action was a tad slower and more methodical than the NHL fare of today, but the sixties game was played by men of steel, determined to do their jobs every night.

The hockey was tremendous to watch, and many fans knew the names of all the 120 players. Individuals became forever associated with one team, and there was no free agency to worry about. Fans could follow the game easily, and the *Hockey Night in Canada* television broadcast on Saturday night was a coast-to-coast event. Nearly everything stopped for the hockey game. Fans were concerned only with the battle on the ice.

The 1967-68 season saw a vast change to the game we knew. The NHL instantly doubled in size, and the average skill level of the players began to drop. Subsequent league expansions have only exacerbated the problem. Much of the "action" now involves hooking, holding and interference (although in the 1997-98 season the league did promise to clean this up). Most teams slap the puck into a corner and then scramble after it. Fighters are now in vogue because coaches try to use intimidation as a strategy. In the sixties, any player who could be intimidated was soon looking for another line of work.

In the process of expanding, hockey has become more international and less tied to its Canadian roots. In the sixties, the majority of the players, coaches and managers were Canadian born. The NHL has sought new franchise locations in faraway places in the United States and has imported new players from Sweden, Finland, Russia and Czechoslovakia. The league's head office, under the guidance of a Canadian-born president, Clarence Campbell, moved from Montreal to New York in 1977 and is now under the power of an American-born commissioner, Gary Bettman. The Canadian cities of Vancouver, Winnipeg, Edmonton, Calgary, Quebec City and Ottawa eventually gained entry into the NHL, but two of these cities no longer have big-league hockey, and other Canadian clubs threaten to leave for cities in the United States that have little interest in hockey. Small-town Canada, once the backbone of the game, has a difficult time surviving in the big money game that the NHL has become.

There is no doubting the skill of the European stars of today's NHL (such as Jaromir Jagr, Pavel Bure, Peter Forsberg and Teemu Selanne) — in fact, many of the leading scorers on any team were born overseas. Canadians first became aware of European talent in 1972, when the Russian team proved that it could compete with Canada's best professional hockey players. In 1980 we witnessed the American Olympic team pull off a miraculous upset of the top Russians, and in 1996 we saw the United States come out on top in the first World Cup of Hockey Tournament (with stars such as Keith Tkachuk, Chris Chelios, Brian Leetch, John LeClair and Mike Richter), beating the Canadian team in the deciding game. The American influence in hockey has certainly come a long way since the mid-sixties, when Boston forward Tom Williams was the only American-born player in the NHL. Yet Canada continues to produce some of the greatest players in the NHL, including Wayne Gretzky, Mario Lemieux, Patrick Roy, Raymond Bourque, Brendan Shanahan, Mark Messier, Eric Lindros and Steve Yzerman.

As great as these players are, they undoubtedly play in a different era. They excel in a time when the third- and fourth-line players form the character of most NHL teams and when there is virtually no chance that the stars will be replaced. The players of the sixties had something to fear: losing their meagre-paying jobs. They played more often for the love of the game than for the almighty dollar (a contract of $100,000 a year was unheard of until the decade was nearly over).

That's why many hockey fans remember the sixties with great fondness and why they never tire of hearing or reading about the epic battles between the "original six" in the last hurrah of great hockey. It's also why the records of Gordie Howe, Bobby Hull, Frank Mahovlich, Dave Keon, Johnny Bower, Glenn Hall, Jean Béliveau, Henri Béliveau Stan Mikita, Jacques Plante, Tim Horton, Norm Ullman, Terry Sawchuk and Bobby Orr are more than the numbers. Their statistics and awards speak of a time of extraordinary men that we are not likely to see again. We can thank gifted artist Harold Barkley for having captured these legends in photographs that will remind us of their superior achievements for many years to come.

Acknowledgements

The author wishes to thank Gino Granieri and Paul Patskou for the use of their research materials; Steve Dryden at *Hockey News* for the use of quotations from back issues of the newspaper, as well as from the sister publications *Hockey World* and *Hockey Pictorial* magazines; Stephen Ciacciarelli of *Hockey Illustrated* for the use of quotations from back issues of the magazine; Michael Carroll, who believed in this book; Brian Scrivener at Raincoast Books for his guidance; and most of all my wife, Maria Leonetti, for all her help, support and understanding.